"To all the people who suffer from the symptoms and misunderstandings of social suffering to suffer amaxophobia "

Index

Introduction

Although the author has previously published two books on phobias *(1. Amaxophobia: how to teach to overcome the fear of driving, and; 2. How to overcome phobias: A guide to learn to overcome irrational fears and the anxiety that accompanies them)*, the present work focuses specifically on theevaluation, diagnosis and treatment of fear of driving.

To achieve these objectives, you will find in the following pages: a) A guide on how to conduct an interview to determine whether we are dealing with a case of rational fearof driving, due to lack of experience, or irrational fear of driving known as amaxophobia. In addition to the interview,you will find a questionnaire that aims to establish thediagnosis, to determine whether we are facing a true case ofamaxophobia or not. Then, having applied the CEVEMICprogram in many cases over the last few years, *we* have beenable to offer you a revised and improved version of the treatment published in the book "S. Sánchez and J. Sánchez (2009). *Amaxophobia: How to teach to overcome the fear ofdriving*".

The aim of this book is to provide people suffering from irrational fear of driving with a guide to help them overcometheir amaxophobia. In the same way, both psychology and psychiatry professionals, as well as road training teachers, can find in this book a new formula to work in tandem, to offer people suffering from this specific type of fear, a greatereffectiveness in the treatment and, when the time comes, a better optimization of safety, when the intervention process requires that the amaxophobic person faces his fear in the "live exposure" phase (real circulation on roads open totraffic).

Following the line raised in the previous paragraph, you will find in this reading: strategies, techniques and resources related to the diagnostic evaluation and treatment derived from the intervention of practical cases of different clinical pictures directly related to the fear of driving.

Both the diagnostic evaluation and the treatment have as a frame of reference theoretical models based on psychological approaches, which have demonstrated, throughout the history of psychology, the achievement of optimal results in the remission of phobias. Specifically, the Cognitive Behavioralmodel and Neuro Linguistic Programming or PNL. In all the cases in which we have intervened, over more than 15 years of experience, the different techniques have been adapted totreat more efficiently the irrational fear of driving, increasingly known as amaxophobia.

Similarly, and in order to remain on the path of science, we will briefly present three articles published by the same author who subscribes this guide, in the journal Securitas Vialis: in the first one, the questionnaire for the evaluation of fear of driving *(Validation of the CEMIC Questionnaire, year 2011)* is validated and made reliable[1]; in the second one *(Evaluation of fear of driving or amaxophobia in pre-drivers, year 2012)*[2], it is found that amaxophobia is present in 19% of the population of people who are obtaining a drivinglicense, and; in the third article *(Evaluation of theeffectiveness of a program designed to overcome fear of driving or amaxophobia, year 2014)*[3]. The results of the research show that the intervention to treat amaxophobia, following the CEVEMIC program, has been effective in 85.7%of the cases studied.

To follow a sequential, structural and pedagogical order, we will start with the definition of the concept of phobia in order to clarify the difference between: 1) Irrational fear (phobia) that can occur in situations or things that are harmless or innocuous, for example, the irrational fear of wearing clothes with buttons, and 2) Rational fear of, for example, entering a lion's cage, which has the function of keeping us away from real dangers to preserve our life and by extension to ensure the continuity of our species.

Although, as we have mentioned, the treatment is based on

---

[1] For more information see: S. Sánchez (2011). Validation of a brief questionnaire for the assessment of fear of driving in pre-drivers. *Securitas Vialis Magazine* 9, 33-48. (2011). Retrieved from https://www.infona.pl/resource/bwmeta1.element.springer-99644a78-b77c-38bb-871b-438e8ca6d116_

[2] More information see article: Sánchez, S. (2012). Assessment of fear of driving or amaxophobia in pre-drivers. *Securitas Vialis*. Retrieved from https://www.infona.pl/resource/bwmeta1.element.springer-5719ff30-faa4-332c-b36f-a9a1ac3b4435

[3] See more in: Sanchez, S. (2014). Evaluation of the effectiveness of a program designed to overcome fear of driving or amaxophobia. Securitas Vialis. Retrieved from https://www.researchgate.net/publication/319134321_Evaluating_the_effectiveness_of_a_program_designed_to_overcome_the_fear_of_driving_or_am axophobia

psychological models and theories, it is not our intention to repeat here the theoretical arguments that have been widely explained in the books and articles published and alluded to in previous lines, although it is true that we will againemphasize the techniques and strategies that support: a) theinterview and the CEMIC questionnaire as tools for the evaluation of amaxophobia and; b) the treatment underlying the CEVEMIC program. The intention is to present succinctlythe theoretical section and take the opportunity to develop the ideas presented through case studies, which we have been dealing with over years of intervention in cases and casehistories directly related to fear of driving. Logically, in orderto preserve the identity of the people we have treated over the years, the names of the characters have been modified, as well as any personal data that could give clues to their identification, presenting, however, the particular descriptionof each of the diagnostic evaluations, accompanied by their corresponding specific treatments and the individual qualitative results.

From the different cases you will have information and knowledge about how amaxophobia (like any other phobia) affects: 1) The cognitive aspects of the person (their ideas, beliefs, thoughts...,); 2) Their behavior (avoiding or fleeing from the phobic stimulus); Their physiological state, where anxiety plays a starring role and protagonist manifesting symptoms such as muscle tension, chest pain, paresthesia (tingling in hands or feet), accelerated heart rate, etc., etc...

Anxiety, as we mentioned in the previous paragraph, will be one of the great stars of this book, since it is the way in which irrational fear manifests itself.

Being anxiety, in most cases, the main cause of the fear to grow exponentially, of course, progressively the phobic person (in this case amaxophobic) ends up developing morefear of his own fear ("fear of being afraid" to "fear of suffering anxiety") than to the fact of driving, or to wear clothes with buttons, or to see a plate with olives ....

*"The only thing we have to fear
is fear as such".*
Franklin D. Roosevelt [4]

Chapter 1

1 *Concept of phobia and amaxophobia*

Phobias are characterized by an irrational and disproportion-ate fear of exposure to situations, places, people, animals, or objects, before which the subject feels helpless and unable to control his behavior and, therefore, tooffer an adequate response that frees him from his fear and discomfort. In gen-eral, the responses selected by people suffering from any type of phobia are avoidance - avoiding the phobic situation - or, in the case of a surprise presentationof the phobic stim-ulus, the subject reacts by quickly moving away from the sit-uation. In both ways they manage to reduceanxiety symp-toms (avoiding or fleeing).

The phobic situation and the avoidance response produce a cycle in which exposure to what is feared reinforces the emo-tion of fear and this in turn generates a constant worry, so that the person who flees from a phobic situation will also avoid it in the future. The consequence of this behavior is that, without knowing it, the person is feeding his fear so it will be more and more difficult for him to face the situations, places, people, animals or objects that provoke this subjec-tive and irrational fear.

1.1 Concept of amaxophobia

Although the term amaxophobia is a neologism that has ap-peared since the second half of the 20th century, from an etymological point of view, the word comes from joining two Greek words: *"Hámaxa"*, which means armor or chassis of a cart or wagon and *"Phobia"*, which has the meaning of fleeing, running away, panic...

---

[4] Franklin D. Roosevelt (1882 - 1945). Politician and lawyer. He was thethirty-second president of the USA, between 1933 and 1945.

The symptoms of phobias manifest themselves at the cognitive, behavioral and physiological levels:

A- Cognitive symptoms are presented by thoughts, ideas and beliefs that cause the person to speculate that something horrible may happen to him/her related to the phobic exposure. The subject evaluates normal situations as threatening and dangerous. An example could be: thinking (in a ruminative[5] way) that: if he/she enters an elevator a respiratory or cardiac arrest will occur. Curiously, the person is more concerned about suffering hyperventilation, or thinking that his heart will accelerate uncontrollably, than believing that the elevator may fall. Making true the premise that one ends up developing fear of fear itself.

B- Some of the most common physiological responses include: sweating, increased muscle tension, increased heart rate, tremors, chest pain, dry mouth, upsetstomach, hyperventilation, numbness of limbs(paresthesia), vomiting, feeling of imminent fainting, etc. The problem is that these anxiety responses, whichin origin may have a preparatory function to provide adaptive responses to a threat, can be associated withnew neutral stimuli that in the future will cause the same physiological symptoms to recur, even in the absence of a real threat.

C- At the behavioral level, the person stops behaving in a normal way, since fear, for example, can cause muscular paralysis that prevents him/her from carryingout any type of task or activity normally, or it could happen that his/her primary reaction is to flee, withoutpaying attention to standard social behavior. In some cases, as in the fear of driving or amaxophobia, the anxiety responses: muscular tension, tachycardia, or the feeling that something horrible is going to happen can lead to the behavior of stopping the vehicle, withouttaking safety precautions, creating a situation of extreme risk by hindering the traffic, or getting out of the vehicle wildly, without adopting due caution, to flee from the situation and thus avoid the aversive anxiogenic

---

[5] Ruminative thinking is characterized by being disorganized and inconsistent. It is full of questions and answers without order and without logic, making it difficult for the person to find adaptive and useful answers

Sebastián Sánchez Marín

symptoms.

Concretizing points A, B and C in a case of amaxophobia wecould observe that:

A. The cognitive symptoms of an amaxophobic are usually: ruminative and anticipatory thinking about the possibility of having an accident. They think that, if the anxiety symptoms associated with their fear occur, they will not be able to maintain control of the vehicle. The truth is that, in this case, the danger may be real, since the situation in which a person is afraid of using an elevator has nothing to do with being afraid of driving a car. In the first case, if someone suffers a panic attack to get into an elevator, the intensity of the anxiety symptoms can cloud their vision, hinder their ability to process information from their environment (they say they are in a kind of cloud that hinders their understanding and movements) and, in many cases, there is difficulty or psychomotor blockade (clumsinessor immobility in legs and arms). As I said, if all this happens to you in an elevator the worst that canhappen is that you have a bad time, because anxiety alone will not cause death, no matter how bad you havea bad time, but if these same symptoms occur when you are responsible for the controls of a vehicle, the situation is very different ... How can you safely handlethe movement of a machine when your eyesight is blurred or muscle tension stiffens your arms or legs?

This situation marks a substantial difference between the treatment of a "normal" phobia and amaxophobia, because in the real exposure (do not worry later we will explain at length what this real exposure is), you can ask a person, who suffers from fear of elevators, to leave the office, to try to enter the elevator and to go up and down the time that is necessary to verify the result of the treatment, but.... In the case of amaxophobia it may be foolhardy to tell someone, whosuffers from panic of driving on highways, to get in their vehicle, to try entering a highway or freeway to see what happens. Even if the psychology professional takes the risk of accompanying this person, who suffers from this very specific type of phobia, it would be irresponsible, unless it is done with a vehicle that has an approved dual control system of brake, clutch and

accelerator installed, in case it is necessary, in a situation of uncontrolled anxiety, to take charge of the
movement of the vehicle.

As you can see, the intervention becomes more complicated, since not all psychology professionals have at
their disposal a vehicle with dual control, and ifso, it is
likely that they do not have the training, or theappro-
priate accreditation, to be able to operate the auxiliary
pedals safely. It is for this reason that in the treatment
of amaxophobia, the joint andcomplementary work of
a psychologist and a roadsafety teacher is essential and
necessary. We will arguethis issue in more detail later
on.

The physiological responses of people who are afraid ofdriving do not differ from those who suffer from other phobias,
only that, as we have explained above, if yourarms or legs
are blocked when you get into an elevator,the problem will
not go much further, but if you suffer a muscle block when
you are driving, I think it is clear that we have increased the
level of real risk a few levels(we may suffer a traffic accident).

Behavioral response of the amaxophobic person: As inany
other phobia, drivers with fear of driving avoid thephobic situation (driving on highways, or going throughtunnels, or on
roads without shoulders, etc.) and, if they cannot avoid it,
then they will try to flee from thesituation that causes them
fear, anxiety and therefore discomfort. The difference, as in
point A (cognitive symptoms of amaxophobia), is the situation. I can avoid going up in elevators or running away from
them,but it can become more than tedious to travel kilometers of urban roads and secondary roads, to avoid using highways or freeways. Even worse if we talkabout fleeing from
them, because once inside a highway it is not so easy to get
out, as we all know thatboth the entrances and exits of this
type of roads are distanced from each other. This circumstance causes the amaxophobic person to panic as he/she is
subjectedto the impossibility of escaping, of fleeing, from the
phobic stimulus. This scenario triggers their anxiety, generating a serious situation of danger, as their behavior
may be to slow down at abnormally lowspeeds for this type
of road or, in the worst case, whenthe anxiety peak is high,
they may stop abruptly in themiddle of the lane they are
driving in.

Possibly, if we illustrate all this theoretical information with a practical case, we will facilitate the reader's understanding of how someone with a fear of driving lives the phobic experience.

Manel and his fear of driving in tunnels

Manel: First part

Manel lives in Girona, he comes to consult because a teacher of road safety training in his town has passed him thetelephone number of our Training and Psychology Center (CFORP) located in the town of Viladecans (Barcelona).

Development of the interview
a) Initial approach or moment

At the beginning of the interview, we ask Manel to describe the problem, how long he has been suffering from it, what he has done so far to solve it and what expectations he has in relation to what is happening to him.

Manel tells us that for the last two years he has been panicking about going through tunnels, especially long ones. He tells us *"I don't know what triggered all this, but now just the thought of having to go through a tunnel makes my heart race like a lawnmower"*. The solutions he has practiced, so far, have not been effective, because at first, to control the anxiety, his family doctor prescribed Diazepam, but as we all knowbenzodiazepines are contraindicated for driving. The second solution turns Manel's work trips into real odysseys, since, if he knows he has to go to Zaragoza,for example, he studies a priori all the possible routes to avoid going through tunnels.

b) Exploration or central moment of the interview

We asked Manel to give us more information about everything that goes through his head before starting new routes, where he does not know if he is going to find tunnels, and/or itineraries, where, yes or yes, he will not be able to avoid entering and circulating through some of those tunnels that he fears so much (we want to investigate in A. Cognitive symptoms).

He tells us that, a few days before starting the trip, he

15

is already nervous, he imagines himself driving through the tunnel, suffering from anxiety and with no possibility of escape (A. Cognitive level), especially if heknows that the tunnel has no shoulders or emergency areas, to be able to stop in case the symptoms are so unbearable that they force him to stop. Manel's anxietysymptoms manifest themselves with a muscular blockage, starting with numbness in his fingers and followed by progressive stiffness in his arms. All this isaccompanied by an increasing horrible tightness in thethoracic plexus (B. Physiological level). As he recounts his thoughts, his nervousness becomes visible, he keeps moving his car keys, which he has left on the table, and he does not seem to find the accommodationhe is looking for in the chair where he is sitting. We askhim why he does not stop moving and his answer is clear: *"As we are talking about tunnels..., I try not to let the stiffness of my hands and arms get the better ofme".*

He goes on to say *"Imagine what could happen if in the middle of the tunnel I can't continue and I have to stop and occupy the lane... I don't even want to think about it".* I ask him if he has ever had to stop his vehicle in the middle of a tunnel lane and... his answer is *"Nooooo!" "God forbids!".* You might be thinking: if you have never been in that situation, why are you so afraid of a situation that hasn't happened to you yet? Perhaps if we analyze your question, we will find the answer. The key is in the **yet**, because he thinks that, although it has not happened to him..., it will happen to him for sure. That, although he has not yet been totally stiffened in any of the situations he has experienced, the next time, his muscular tension will be such that hewill suffer a blockage, so that, before losing absolute control, he will have to stop his vehicle, without the possibility of moving it to the shoulder, with the danger that this action entails. He tells me that all thesethoughts flood his head a few days before leaving on atrip, so he has a very hard time falling asleep and whenhe does, he wakes up startled by nightmares that are fed by the same insidious, recurrent and ruminating thought. Then, what he does is to look for alternativesto avoid confrontation (avoidance) or to escape from his fear (flight). Thus, he may spend all night looking for secondary road itineraries, which can add kilometers, time and discomfort to his travels. All to avoid suffering again from the fear of losing control, thus feeding their fear of being afraid (fear of fear).

Your face and your story denote dejection. I tell you not to worry that everything has a solution and that precisely one of the areas where psychology has takengiant steps is in the treatment of phobias, so once we have a clear diagnosis and your level of phobia, helped by the questionnaire to assess the fear of driving (CEMIC Questionnaire) we will start an appropriate and specific treatment tailored to this particular fear, which suffers, known as amaxophobia.

c) Conclusion or final moment of the interview

We conclude the interview by summarizing everything that has been discussed, establishing a plan of the objectives we want to achieve and the order we are going to follow in the intervention:

a) Passing the CEMIC questionnaire (initial evaluation)
b) Knowing fear and its functionality
c) Differentiating between rational fear andirrational fear
d) Describe and apply the visualization exposure technique in imagination.
e) Culminate the treatment with actual exposure
f) Verify the results of the intervention byadministering the CEMIC again (final evaluation).

Do not worry if many of the things I have described in the list of objectives, which I have just presented to you, do not ring a bell or you do not know them. Throughout the reading of this book, you will see that you will find more profuse and detailed definitions that will clarify your doubts or questions. Now that you know Manel and how the initial interview went, maybe it's time for us to continue in the "Concept of phobia" thread.

1.2 What is fear and what is it for?

Fear is a primary emotion and despite how annoying it may seem, it is part of our survival system, it is as old as life and its function is to preserve our physical integrity and by extension to safeguard the species. We have to differentiate fear from anxiety, as they are often two terms that are confused or used in an analogous way.

Fear is the emotion that arises when we are faced with danger, while anxiety is the adaptive response of our organism to that danger, or risk situation. The fear-anxiety binomial manifests itself (as mentioned in the introduction) at a cognitive, physiological and behavioral level. Its function is to set in motion defense mechanisms that allow us to escape unharmedfrom threatening situations.

In the face of a threat, our whole organism prepares itself to offer two possible responses: fight or flight. In either case, our muscles tense up and receive more oxygen and glucose, our attention increases, our heart pumps harder to supply blood to the vital organs and especially to the brain (we need to think fast), we breathe faster in order to provide oxygen to our lungs, our pupils dilate in order to widen our angle of vision and, we go into a state of alertness ranging from mild to high alert depending on our perception of the degree of danger to which we believe we are exposed.

1.3 Rational versus irrational fear

1.3.1 Rational fear

It is innate, it is part of our phylogenetic inheritance and it is necessary to preserve the species. If we put a small child to crawl on a table, it will crawl in all possible directions. When it reaches an edge, it will become aware of the danger and take another direction. If we are walking in the countryside one day and suddenly, we realize that we are inside an enclosure where there are wild bulls and one of them looks at us, digs into the ground with one of its legs, and immediately starts running towards us, no doubt fear will not leave us impassive, it will trigger a state of alert, which will make us react by setting in motion the appropriate anxiety mechanism to flee, in haste, from the scene of danger. It could also be that fear leaves us petrified, in a state of tonic immobility[6]. This circumstance is another possible response to extreme situations: muggings, serious accidents, aggressions, rapes...

---

[6] Tonic immobility or thanatosis is a defense mechanism used by some animals such as the brown snake (Storeria dekayi), the lemon shark, the opossum (...), when faced with threatening situations in which they knowthat if they confront their adversary, they have no chance of winning

In the same way, in the city we are surrounded by dangers. The traffic and the circulation of vehicles can constitute a great risk for the possibility of suffering an accident: there are visual stimuli such as a stop sign; or auditory stimuli such as the "Horn" of a vehicle that make us activate the mentioned alert. If for example we are about to cross a street on foot and at that moment we hear the sustained sound of a "Horn", instinctively we are assaulted by the emotion of fear, alertness and anxiety are activated, in order to sharpen our senses, we will react by directing our attention towards the stimulus and we will make a quick jump (adaptive response) that will save us from danger.

As mankind has evolved, dangers (and consequently fears) have changed. In ancient times, due to the precariousness and insecurity of the hostile environment where daily life developed, fears arose mostly in the face of dangers that werereal, such as *"the fear of being devoured by an animal"*. Currently the evolution of society has preserved us from suchdangers, but an even greater fear has arisen, if possible, whichis the fear of losing that security ... Too many changes, everything happens too fast. These incessant and fulminant changes cause us insecurity in our social, work and couple relationships.

Currently, in Bauman's words,[7] we find ourselves in a liquid society. We have lost solidity and stability: at work, with our partner, with our friends. All this feeling of instability makes us afraid of not being competent, of not being loved, of being rejected in the work, family, personal, social world and in the end, it makes us end up in a spiral where *"we are afraid of our own fear"*, *"we are afraid to be afraid and to suffer itssymptoms"*. From this fear of being afraid (fear of fear itself) irrational fears (phobias) arise and take hold.

1.3.2 Irrational fear

It is characterized by a distorted perception of the threat, since we either imagine a danger that has no basis, or we magnify the consequences of exposure to a situation, person, animal or thing. It would be a fear that is not justified by any previous experience or knowledge, but by our anticipation and mental elaboration of negative consequences of exposing ourselves to the phobic stimulus. Let's clarify it a little more with an

---

[7] Zygmunt Bauman (1925-2017): born in Poland. Sociologist, philosopher andessayist. He developed the concept of liquid modernity.

example.

If we manifest fear in the presence of a wild animal, let's say for example a lion, we would say that it is a rational fear, it is possible that we have had a real previous experience on a trip to the African savannah, where our life was in danger, or that we have seen a documentary, or read, or heard that the lion is a predator that attacks people.... But if the fear is triggered by the sight of a plate of olives, we could assure that it is an irrational fear, since it is unlikely that someone has been attacked by an olive and, although the person may think thathe could choke if he consumes it, it is improbable that the olive takes the initiative to move towards his mouth and, if so, the probability that it could cause death by choking is not higher than that of any other type of food, of those that can be consumed daily.

Anxiety is nourished, to a great extent, by our **anticipation of the results** of facing what we fear. In phobias there is a closed loop of fear and avoidance, which means that, by refusing to face the phobic stimulus, we cannot get out of that circle. So that: - *"If I do not confront my fear, I get it to progressively increase to the point where it affects the normal performance of my life."* In fact, phobias, or irrational fears, gain or lose importance depending on how disabling they can be, for example: if I am afraid of elevators and I live and work in first floor buildings, it does not matter much if I have or do not have that kind of phobia, but if I work in a 30-story building and I am responsible for distributing office supplies between the 1st and 30th floor..., it seems that my problem has gone up a few steps in the field of importance. It has become disabling.

1.4 More or less known phobias

There are many and varied phobias that we could talk about in this section. Some of them are better known, more shared and public, since the person who suffers from them does not feel bad or is not ashamed when it is said that he/she suffers from them. This would be the case of claustrophobia (fear of enclosed spaces), to other more rare and covert phobias, since the person tries to hide the fact that he/she suffers from it, since he/she thinks that nobody will understand what is happening to him/her, that he/she will feel ridiculous and that he/she is a freak. This could be the case of trypophobia (fear of holes when they are together, as in bee panels, or holes in a brick...). In general, it is not unusual to find someone who says they are afraid of enclosed spaces, who tells you that they suffer from claustrophobia, but it is quite rare forsomeone to confess that they are trypophobic, so if you showthem a sink grate, full of holes, they will run away without explaining why they are running away.

To get a small idea of the quantity and variety of irrational fears, or phobias, that we can find, we are going to present a small list of them, which, as you can imagine, is not exhaustive by any means. The list is divided into two typologies: one composed of those phobias that are somewhat better known and others that are not so well known. The point is that later on you will see that it doesn't matter in which list you find the phobia you know or suffer from, because they all share the same territory.

Even if your irrational fear is not included in any of the lists do not worry, because the treatment steps are similar in all cases, you just have to adapt it to the phobia, to the specific symptoms of anxiety, and to the idiosyncrasy of the person who suffers from it.

1.4.1 Most known phobias

a. **Phobia of flying**: phobia characterized by the fear of flying. Currently, many airlines offer courses and treatments to overcome the fear of flying, and even have established intervention plans in case any of their passengers suffer an anxiety crisis due to this irrational fear.

b. **Phobia of heights**: or fear of heights, is one of the most common phobias among human beings. They suffer from fear at the mere thought of looking out of a window, going out onto a balcony.... Impossible for them to go zip-lining, paragliding, parachute jumping..., just thinking about it produces anincapacitating and paralyzing vertigo.

c. **Agoraphobia**: The fear of open spaces, crowds, queues, the use of public transport, or any other place where people congregate such as shopping malls.Going to one of these places usually becomes a nightmare for agoraphobic people, so they will avoid them at all costs.

d. **Spider phobia**: also suffered by many people, who feel anxiety at the mere sight or thought of a spider, so they will avoid going to gardens, country houses, or any other place where they suspect there may be any type of arachnid.

e. **Phobia of storms**: These people are afraid of storms, lightning, thunder, lightning. In some cases, people who suffer from claustrophobia, before a storm, hide in any closet, under a bed ...

f. **Needle phobia**: many people are afraid of needles or any other sharp object. This situation becomes a real problem when it is necessary to have a blood extraction, a surgical intervention, etc.

g. **Dog phobia**: people suffering from this phobia show anxiety and fear before any type of dog, be it big, small, dangerous or harmless.

h. **Claustrophobia**: perhaps one of the most popular and well-known phobias. Fear of enclosed spaces (elevators, car interiors, etc.) generally suffer from the sensation of suffocation.

i. **Phobia of blood**: better known as fear of blood. We allknow people who, if they see blood or you simply talk to them about something related to blood, may feel sick, dizzy, and may even faint.

j. **Button phobia**: although at first glance it may not seem like a known phobia, the truth is that it is much more common than it seems. People who suffer from this phobia are people who panic about buttons, so on their clothes you can find any type of closure (, zippers, hooks, lac-es ...), everything except buttons.

k. **Phobia of darkness**: more present and common in early ages (children), it usually manifests itself at night, since it is an exacerbated fear of darkness.

1.4.2 **Lesser-known phobias**

a. **Coulrophobia**: irrational fear before the presence of a clown, or acts or places where it is suspected that it may appear.

b. **Phobia of clowns**: people suffering from this phobia are afraid of money. Specifically, to the impact that money can have on their life. To have or not to have money. It is related to wealth or poverty, to social status... To be loved for the money you possess and not for what you are... This phobia has nothing to do with touching or not touching money, but with what is associatedand related to money: power, corruption, domination...

c. **Phobia of trees**: irrational fear of trees, bushes and forests. Although this phobia is more prevalent inchildren, it is also observed in adults.

d. **Phobia of long or difficult words**: it is curious that the term attributed to this particular phobiais a word so long and complex, because people suffering from this phobia are precisely afraid of long orcomplicated words to pronounce, especially when theyhave to use them in a meeting or event that they consider important.

e. **Rainwater phobia**: intense and uncontrollable fear of getting wet with rainwater. These people may accumulate a multitude of objects or utensils to avoid getting wet in the rain (umbrellas, raincoats, tarpaulins, awnings...).

f. **Phobia to see a navel**: these people show fear and dread atthe possibility of having to see a navel and even more so if they had to touch it. This includes their own navel,so you can imagine how complicated it can be to take abath or shower.

g. **Phobia of beards**: people who suffer from this phobia are afraid of beards, the longer and thicker they are, the more aversion and nausea they feel.

h. **Sleep phobia**: this phobia is a real health problem because people who suffer from it are afraid of sleeping. Sleep is necessary and unavoidable. Imagine the suffering of someone who is terrified of falling asleep, because they think that during sleep, they may suffer acardiac arrest, respiratory arrest, etc. They are afraid of not waking up again.

i. **Phobia of objects with symmetrical holes**: the fear of these people concentrates onany object that contains holes together. For example, ahoneycomb or holes in a brick.

j. **Cheese phobia**: or fear of cheese, not only the presence of cheese, but also its smell, produces nausea and a feeling of intense discomfort in people suffering from this phobia.

k. **Phobia of the color yellow**: irrational fear of the color yellow.These people react with anxiety to any object containing the color yellow. In some cases, even hearing the word "yellow" is enough to cause an anxiety crisis.

As mentioned above, this list is a small sample of the myriadof phobias we could talk about.

1.5 Response to a phobic stimulus

In general, the response that a person will express to a situation that causes phobia, for example: In a case of cynophobia (fear of dogs) it will be ...

a. Avoidance behavior: Try, as far as possible, to AVOID encountering the phobic stimulus that causes anxiety symptoms. In this case, you will avoid going to places where there may be dogs.

b. FLIGHT behavior: If exposure to the phobic situation has not been avoided, they will flee. For example: A person when turning a corner sees in the distance that a neighbor, whom she knows, is walking her dog on the same sidewalk that she occupies. The neighbor sees this person, turns and goes to meet her. In this case, the cynophobic will choose to be in evidence with the neighbor and, pretending to be clueless, will cross the sidewalk, or turn around suddenly, in order to escape, to flee, from the stimulus (the dog) that causes him fear and anxiety.

In general, the response that a person will manifest in a situation that provokes a phobia, for example: In a case of cynophobia (fear of dogs) will be...

   a. **Avoidance behavior**: Try, as far as possible, to AVOID encountering the phobic stimulus that causes the anxiety symptoms. In this case, avoid going to places where dogs may be present.

   b. **Flight behavior**: If the exposure to the phobic situation could not be avoided, the person will flee. Forexample: A person turning a corner sees in the distance that a neighbor, whom she knows, is walkinghis dog on the same sidewalk she occupies. The neighbor sees this person, turns around and goes to meet him. In this case, the person who has a phobia of dogs will choose to expose himself to the neighbor and, pretending to be distracted, will cross the sidewalk, or will turn suddenly, to escape, to flee from the stimulus (the dog) that it causes fear and anxiety.

*"Where the waterreaches its
greatest depth,
is calmer".*
William Shakespeare [8]

Chapter 2

2 Concept of anxiety

According to the Royal Spanish Academy, anxiety (in its first meaning) is a state of agitation, restlessness or anxiety of the spirit. It also tells us (in its second meaning) that anxiety is a state of anguish that usually accompanies many diseases, particularly certain neuroses, andthat does not allow patients to rest.

But, and in the field, we are dealing with...

2.1 What is anxiety and what is it for?

Anxiety is an adaptive response that follows the emotion of fear in a situation that may be threatening. Some people confuse anxietythinking that it is just another emotion, as could be joy, fear, anger orsadness, but it is not.

Anxiety has to do with the anticipation of any imminent or future real danger, so it can be of great help to avoid avoidable risks.

I am going to try to expose the difference and the existing utility (yes, yes, I said utility) between fear and anxiety on condition that you join me in the following fable:

Our ancestor Ju the troglodyte

Imagine going back to the time when our ancestors hunted with stone axes, wore skins and shared the water they consumed with the local wildlife. In general, they would get their water from a river, lake or pond near the place where they lived or had decided to set up camp.

Now, he continues to imagine that Ju, our troglodyte friend, is the new man in charge of supplying the village with water. It is a job that fills him with pride and satisfaction, because it is not a job that the chief of the tribe leaves in the hands of

---

[8] William Shakespeare (1564 - 1616). British writer.

just anyone? On the other hand, he is a bit worried because his predecessor, in the position he is about to occupy, has just been eaten by a wild animal.

When the time comes, Ju adjusts to his shoulders an implement made of a branch, from the ends of which hang two ropes that hold a kind of cauldron on each side. As he moves away from the safety of his village, he notices how hismuscles tense. As he feels his heart in his mouth, it is clear to him that everything is a product of his fear, fear that whathappened to his predecessor might happen to him, but his pride is stronger and pushes him to continue.

A few meters before reaching the pond, he sharpens his hearing in order to discriminate any variation of noise, either by excess or defect (a strange sound or an unexpected silence could be indicators of danger). He scans with his eyes for possible variations in movement, in color, or in the usual size that corresponds to the vegetation and foliage of the place. He does not know it, but his anxiety is facilitating a better activation of his visual, auditory and even olfactory acuity. It is also anxiety that is providing more glucose and oxygen to his cells in anticipation of a demand for greater muscular effort, whether to go into fight mode, repel an attack, or makea quick getaway. It is anxiety that keeps you in a state of maximum alertness.

Ju is squatting down to fill the second container, just seconds before the water overflows the rim when..., as if pushed by an invisible spring, he has jumped backwards like a leaping gazelle.[9] The sequence lasted tenths of a second. Even so, he could not free himself from a deep wound that will remain forever, as a war trophy, marking his cheek. It will be a certificate of the day he faced an immense and terriblecrocodile in his mission to care for and watch over his people.Only he knows he is alive by the detail of having been alerted,seeing a tiny suspicious ripple in the water, just before seeingthe impressive snout of the monstrous reptile emerge.

2.2 Relationship between fear and anxiety

Once the story is over, the following questions arise:

---

[9] The leaping gazelle inhabits southeastern Africa and, in order to escape frompredators, can leap up to two meters high.

a. What role do you think fear and anxiety have played in Ju's story?

b. Do you think that if Ju had not been afraid of being devoured, the necessary alerts would have been activated so that his anxiety would have provided him with the necessary resources to escape from the crocodile's jaws?

I am probably not wrong in assuming that we agree that fear and anxiety responses, in both scenarios, have been decisive factors in saving Ju's life. This situation leads us to ask ourselves one more question:

c. Do you think the end of our troglodyte's story would have been the same if Ju had been a real passive, carefree and free of fear and anxiety?

What do you think? We agree again! Yes? Of course, we do. Surely if our ancestor Ju had been a person totally free of worries, fears and adaptive responses of anxiety he would not have died of heart attack, or stress, or anything similar but in such a hostile environment and exposed to so many dangers, I can assure you that he would not have reached adulthood, let alone old age, so he would have reduced his chances of mating, of having offspring and by extension to contribute to perpetuate his species (our species), so if we (you and I) would have had a direct relationship in the line of succession of the version of a "passive" Ju... WE WOULD NOT BE HERE.

What I want to tell you is that both fear and anxiety have a function and that is to keep us in a state of alert and activation in order to avoid, or face (if there is no other way), the possible real dangers that may threaten us.

So... Where does that leave us? Is anxiety good or bad for us? Is a fork good or bad for us?

Anxiety is an infallible and necessary resource when it is activated by the emotion of fear motivated by a real threat situation (anxiety is positive when it occurs when it has to occur).

The cases in which anxiety is considered as harmful or pathological arethose associated with the presence of an irrational or illogical fear, andthe anxiety response is unjustified or disproportionate. It would be thecase in which the anxiety response is exaggerated and/or un-controlledby: fear of wearing clothes with buttons, fear of needles, olives, the color yellow, the number 13...

2.3 Symptoms of anxiety

The forms in which the anxiety can manifest itself, before the presence, real or imaginary, of the phobic stimulus are many and varied.Although the fear is of the same thing, for example, fear of the dark not all people present the same symptoms, nor with thesame intensity.

Thus, we can observe people suffering from a single symptom, for example the sensation of choking, precursor of hyperventilation, to those who may present a wider range of unpleasant sensations, some of them associated with imminent death. Thus, within this amplitude of symptomatology we can find, apart from those mentioned above: sensation of numbness or tingling (paresthesia in the extremities or fingertips), tightness in the chest (feeling of having on the chest a great weight, a slab), alteration of the heart rate (usually tachycardia), sensation of heart attack, palpitations, sweating, muscular tension and stiffness, dry mouth, nausea, sensation of dizziness and even fainting, feeling of unreality and in some cases of depersonalization, where the person perceives the situation as if he/she were living it from outside his/her body...

2.4 How to control anxiety

It is curious, not to say paradoxical, to talk about anxiety control on the assumption that: The more attention is paid to anxiety the stronger it becomes and the more its presence time will increase. The terminological problem is that to maintain control over something youhave to pay attention to it. I mean that, to give an example, if you want to control that a baby does not hurt himself when you are helpinghim to take his first steps, you have to pay maximum attention to him,because an absent-mindedness can mean that he ends up face down on the floor. The paradox is that with anxiety, the more you listen to it, the more you want to control it, the more it wants to be with you, the more it grows and the stronger it becomes.

It is for all this that it is complicated to speak of anxiety control because at the very moment that we have decided to exercise control over anxiety we have lost the battle. You just have to remember that anxiety is fed by all the attention that is devoted to it.

To facilitate what I am trying to explain, I would like you to remember the case of Manel and his fear of tunnels. One of the issues that has not been reflected in the brief summary of his initial interview is that Manel remembers that a few days before suffering his first episode of fear while driving through a tunnel, his company was in a difficult situation, as they were adjusting the workforce and Manel thought thatit

30

was very likely that one of the candidates for dismissal would be him. According to him, the situation could not have been more tragic and terrible, as he had just signed the mortgage for his house and was expecting his first baby. Although he was very excited about becoming a father, he was also aware of the great changes that the arrival of a new member of the family would entail... And even more so now, when the uncertainty in his job was putting his finances in the balance. Responsibility and uncertainty do not go well together and this was taking its toll on Manel, increasing his insecurity, stress and anxiety.

2.5 Fear, anxiety, and somatization.

What Manel does not suspect is that the states of fear and anxiety are usually somatized, or what is the same, they manifest and express themselves in physiological symptoms. Remember that in previous pages we have commented that, fear provokes: A. Cognitive symptoms; B. Physiological responses, and; C. Behavioral responses.

If we could look back in the chronology of the events that provoked the fear of the tunnels of Manel we would find that:

1. Manel suffers from stress and anxiety, due to his work and family situation, a few days before his first episode of fear while driving through a tunnel.

2. This situation makes it difficult for him to fall asleep and thus achieve a restorative state of his organism[10].

3. Stress, anxiety and lack of sleep often trigger physiological responses such as: accelerated heart rate, muscle tension, chest tightness, paresthesia in arms and legs, hyperventilation...

This being so, it seems that we are not contributing anything new, but perhaps we should put the focus on the moment when the physiological responses are manifested.

Imagine that Manel is leaving his boss's office. He is pale, he has just found out that this will be his last month in the company... He is looking for a chair to sit on, as he begins to feel an annoying muscular blockage that makes it difficult for him to walk. In addition to the muscular blockage, he is starting to have some difficulty breathing (he feels like

---

[10] When we sleep, sleep goes through five distinct phases. In the last phase (phase 5), the rapid eye movement phase, known as the REM phase (which occurs for the first time between 70 and 90 minutesafter the onset of sleep), is when our brain and our organism recover energy, learning processes are consolidated and energy is rebalanced.

a heavy slab on his chest). A couple of colleagues, who have their desk near the director's office, and who observe the situation, come to help him when they see Manel's depressed state. The question we should ask ourselves is: Do you think Manel's coworkers will understand that sluggish legs and tightness in the chest can be normal physiological responses in anyone who has just been told they are out of a job?

Before you answer, let me ask you a second question Do you think that Manel himself will assimilate his symptoms as natural, after having verified that his worst suspicions have come true?

I guess the answer to the two previous questions is the same: YES, of course, any of us would understand that someone will end up suffering an anxiety crisis in a situation like the one experienced by Manel.

We all understand that an "effect" is usually the result of a "cause", but we are not prepared to find and accept causeless effects that cause it. To explain myself better, let me resort to the allegory, which I have used before, about the pain in a finger... Everyone understands and accepts that a finger hurts if you have just taken a hammer blow. Moreover, this circumstance does not give rise to great concern, since it is accepted that the effect of this pain is caused by the hammer blow. The question posed would have a singularly different appreciation if the pain in the finger appears just like that, without a previous blow, without a twist, without a cause that justifies that pain.

The problem lies in the fact that Manel's first panic attack was not just when he left his boss's office, after seeing that his name had been added to the list of those who had been fired that month. If that had been the case, everyone, along with him, would have understood and accepted as normal that Manel had shown symptoms of anxiety and distress. Everyone would have understood the cause-effect binomial.

The problem is that, at that moment, Manel has not yet assimilated, he is not aware of what awaits him, so that panic attack will be postponed for when his brain has had time to process all that information and, that circumstance, can occur at any time, in any placeand in any situation, for example..., passing through a tunnel. When Manel suffers the first anxiety crisis while going through a tunnel, his mind associates (anchors) the suffered symptoms of anxiety with the tunnel and/or any situation similar or similar to a tunnel.

2.5.1 Etiology and maintenance of Manel's phobia

The point is that in most cases of phobias the onset and process follow the same etiological and somatization pattern, developed in the previous point.

Perhaps to finish understanding the process we need to talk about: the association of ideas (known in Neuro Linguistic Programming as anchoring) and Pavlov's Classical Conditioning (don't worry, in a later chapter we will present these concepts more extensively). Now, if you allow me, let's continue with Manel's story.

Manel and his fear of driving in tunnels

Manel: Second part

> There are just a few days left to finish his work in the company where he has been working for 12 years (all his working life). Manel is on his way to "La Vall d'Aran"[11]. He is going to visit some customers that he may never see again... That moves him emotionally, because they were the first ones who trusted him, at the beginning of his career as a salesman of hotel and catering machinery.
>
> As he drives, his thoughts are constantly racing about how he is going to cope with his new situation. He imagines himself without a job, without income... In the street, after an eviction order from his barely new house... He sees himself with his wife and his newborn baby, living badly in a small room at his parents' house... Perhaps, the economic hardship will end up souring his character and all this will lead to a deterioration in the couple's relationship...
>
> He is arriving at the entrance to the Viella Tunnel (a tunnel he has traveled through at least two or three times a year since he started as a salesman). As he enters the tunnel his thoughts continue to advance, giving way to feelings of fear before the situation that is coming upon him... His life is falling apart... He is more and more convinced that his wife is going to leave him, which means that he will not be able to see or be with his baby as he had always wished and imagined...
>
> Halfway through the tunnel, Manel begins to feel the fingers of his hands start to stiffen, while an incipient feeling of tightness in his chest causes difficulty in breathing...
>
> The process of fear to circulate through the tunnels has just

---

[11] The Vall d'Aran, located in the province of Lleida is a valley of the Pyrenees and at the same time a region of Catalonia.

begun its journey, the **unconscious mind** of Manel is **associating** in this instant: the passage through the **tunnel** with his **anxiety response**, so from now on, just as our ancestor Ju had well associated danger cues, which could be imperceptible to anyone else who was unaware of the context and its risks, Manel has just unconsciously (unknowingly) associated his fear of tunnels with his paired anxiety responses, with the difference that Ju was in a real scenario of danger, so his fear is a conscious, rational and justified fear, while Manel manifests a response of anguish and anxiety provoked by an unconscious and unjustified irrational fear (amaxophobia) of driving through a tunnel. This exacerbated fear that Manel is suffering, at this moment, is not justified because, a priori, there is the same level of general risk in driving (except for specific details), whether you drive on a highway, on a conventional road, or through a tunnel. What I mean is that a driver in normal conditions does not present changes in his anxiety levels due to the fact of driving on an urban or interurban road, or over a bridge, or whether it is night or day, etc., etc.

Perhaps you're planting that in many moments of our life we suffer from anxiety and in principle it does not become a problem.

The truth is that you are absolutely right, but even at the risk of being labeled as "macho" I remind you that when anxiety is presented by a justified origin, and we are aware of what causes it, then it will not go beyond that, because we are facing a case of cause-effect.

Manel would have understood and accepted the symptoms of anxiety, which he is suffering now in the tunnel, if he had experienced them at the moment when he was walking out the door of the office of the director of his company. But now, in the tunnel, his mind does not understand, does not comprehend, does not find the cause of his anxious responses, so the mind chooses to do what it does best, associating details, situations, places (...) to his anxiety and, just as in the tunnel, his mind does not understand, does not understand, does not find the cause of his anxious responses.) to his anxiety and, just as Ju had associated the sound of a small dry gill breaking with the nearby presence of a predator and his anxiety was triggered to tense his muscles in order to jump and run away from a real danger... Manel's mind ends up associating the presence of a tunnel with the trigger of his anxiety, only that, no matter how many times he turns it around, he does not find any rational explanation.
From there, the sequence is:

    a) As soon as Manel knows that he is going to go through a tunnel his worry begins, because he has unconsciously associated tunnels with his fear and anxiety response.

b) Inside, or before reaching the tunnel, Manel will unconsciously be on the lookout for any of his anxiety symptoms. In his case, he is watching to see if he feels any stiffness, however small, in his fingers, or any sign of tightness in his chest.

c) Naturally, he who seeks finds. As Manel is hyper-focused on finding some sign of muscle stiffness, he immediately finds it. The problem is that this stiffness does not necessarily have to be caused by anxiety, but may be due to a postural issue, think about whether it is normal or not that after two or three hours of your foot pressing the accelerator you may feel some slight muscle discomfort and, if you are also in "search mode" then it will be normal that you end up finding what you were looking for.

d) The fact that Manel notices that small sensation of muscular tension in the instep of his right foot causes anxiety to be initiated and maintained (since anxiety feeds on the attention paid to it). As anxiety increases, the symptom of muscle stiffnessin Manel's foot becomes more accentuated, as the symptom becomes more accentuated, anxiety increases... Thus, entering an endless spiral or loop, which does nothing but grow and grow...

e) One of the possible endings of these episodes of fear and anxiety response usually end up in the Emergency Department of the nearest Hospital in the area of the event. Surely, there, after an accurate diagnosis of anxiety crisis, which rules out a possible angina pectoris, or signs of heart attack, you will be prescribed a rescue medication (usually Diazepam), to immediately lower your anxiety state and will be recommended to start a combined treatment of psychology and drugs.

But what would have happened, if in this, or other similar cases, the person suffering from amaxophobia, or any other type of phobia, had not been frightened when feeling the initial symptoms of anxiety? In fact, I am sure that Manel would not have been frightened, nor would he have been afraid of feeling muscular tension or tightness in his chest, if he had felt that anxiety at the very moment, he was leaving his boss's office, after learning of his dismissal.

Moreover, if it is all right with you, let me use the Socratic method[12] to shed some more light on this path, towards knowledge and

---

[12] Socrates (470 BC - 399 BC). He was a philosopher of ancient Greece. He used the method of maieutic (technique of assisting in childbirth, Socrates' mother was a midwife). It consists of achieving, by means of pertinent questions, that people bringout the knowledge they possess within themselves.

understanding of amaxophobia, that we have undertaken together.

a. What do you think would have happened, with Manel's anxiety crisis, if at the first symptom of anxiety (he feels muscular tension in his right foot) it would have been possible to stop paying attention to him?

b. Do you think that if he had stopped concentrating on his symptoms (because he was a passive, or because he had founda justification) he would have ended up in the EmergencyDepartment of a Hospital?

I guess you are clear on both answers, right?

By the way, I have never understood why this benzodiazepine derivative, better known as Valium or Diazepam, is called "rescue medication" in these cases. The truth is that, in certain situations, it can become the direct cause of the panic attack, for example: When you realize that the pill is not where you expected to find it and you are far from getting it.

The figurative sequence could be:

1) You're on the Costa Brava, and you're thinking how beautiful this little town is!

2) Wow, as good as I was, enjoying the day, the sun, the views, the nature, now I seem to start feeling a little tightness in my chest (symptom of anxiety).

3) Well, I don't have to worry, if I see that my nervousnesscontinues to increase, I will take the Diazepam that I always carrywith me, because..., I have taken it, haven't I?

4) I'm going to check that it's in my pocket.

5) My God, I can't find the pill, it's not there, now there's no way to stop the anxiety, in fact, I'm starting to feel the terrible sensation of a heavier and heavier slab on my solar plexus. In fact, I start to feel the terrible sensation of having a heavier and heavier slab in my solar plexus, I notice my difficulty in breathing, God, I'm sweating profusely, my pulse..., I'm dizzy!

Result of this whole episode: Return to the nearest hospital in the area.

2.6 Information as a tool to overcome anxiety

What does not seem easy is to manage not to pay attention to something that worries or frightens us, and the things that worry us most are those that we do not know or those that we are afraid of.

Generally, the less information we have about a new phenomenon, the more worry and anxiety it causes us.

> In a radio interview with María Dolores Pradera[13], at one point the presenter asked María Dolores "How do you deal with the <¡Ays!>" referring to how she dealt with the aches and pains of being an old person. To which she replied - *"Well, you see, I stopped paying attention to my <¡Ays!> some time ago, because what really worries me are my <¡Uys!>"*.
> In response to this answer, the presenter, puzzled, asked María Dolores *"What do you mean?"* and she answered *"Well, I am not afraid of <¡Ays!>, I already know them, I know what they are, for example <¡Ay, my knee hurts again>, however, an <¡Uy!> is very different because it is unknown. An <Oops!> is accompanied by uncertainty... <Oops, this pain in my side that I have never felt before... What could it be?>. An <Oops!> sows in you worry and bewilderment, because it is something that a priori you do not know"*.

The truth is that I was never a big fan of María Dolores, but that day she gained in me a faithful devotee. Devotee of her maturity, of her ability to take advantage of her experience, of her handling of information, and above all of her good use of common sense, which ontoo many occasions is often conspicuous by its absence.

Regarding the good use of knowledge and information: War strategists know very well that the best weapon they can use to defeat their enemy is KNOWLEDGE and INFORMATION. Knowing and knowing about their strengths, their weaknesses, their routines, their way of being, of thinking, of feeling, of reacting? All this compendium of information and knowledge will serve so that the plan to be devised, drawn up and executed to defeat the adversary is practical, safe and effective.

It is for all that has been said so far that I consider that one of the best tools or resources to **overcome fears** (especially if they are irrational) is to know how to **manage anxiety** and the symptoms that derive from it. Not by means of the prescription of a "rescue pill", but from an arduous and therapeutic work that must begin by offering, to who

---

[13] María Dolores Pradera (1924 - 2018). She was born in Madrid. She stood out in show business as a melodic singer and actress.

suffers the phobia, the necessary information with the purpose that the person who suffers it knows in detail:

a) What is anxiety?

b) What is it for?

c) Why, when and how does it occur?

d) What are the strategies and resources to help us manage it?

It is clear that therapy cannot be reduced to offering a huge amount of information, so later we will introduce the strategies, techniques and resources that will help us to overcome irrational fears, but before continuing (in order to avoid confusion or misunderstandings), allow me to make a digression:

> I would not like anyone to think that when I speak of "rescue medication" it should be understood as a criticism of the emergency services of any hospital, but on the contrary, I think that the health personnel who are able to attend, quickly and effectively, patients who present themselves without prior appointment, without knowing a priori what type of pathology or trauma the person who enters the door may have... I sincerely believe that these health professionals should be given a monument.

> In fact (I believe I am not mistaken), the priority objective of an "Emergency Department" is not to perform a diagnostic evaluation in order to establish a treatment, but to manage to attend and, if necessary, stabilize from: a girl who has filled her nostrils with plasticine, to someone who presents a vital risk due to respiratory collapse.

> If we review the case of our friend Manel: he entered the Emergency Department believing he was having a heart attack and left with the feeling that it had all been a bad dream that was finally over. If his anxiety level dropped from 10 (to give an example on a numerical scale) to 3. For me, the Emergency Department achieved its priority objective (in this case: to stabilize the patient's anxiety).

> From this point on, it is Manel's **responsibility to** seek professional help in order to initiate a concrete treatment tailored to a specific and thorough diagnostic evaluation.

Continuing with the idea of not paying too much attention to anxiety, to prevent it from feeding on our attention, and thus keep growing and growing until it becomes an uncontrollable monster, let me share with you the metaphor that I usually tell my patients in consultation about anxiety.

Mrs. Pepita

Pepita is my neighbor in Quinto B, we share the staircase landing. Pepita is not a bad person, in fact, she is always looking out for me, she makes sure I don't get cold, that I don't get constipated, that my hair is straight and aligned, that my shoes are shiny... I don't know very well how she finds out what happens to me, but she finds out and comes immediately to tell me to wrap up warm, to comb my hair, or to give more shine to my shoes...

Yesterday, without going any further, I was engrossed in preparing some fried eggs and I got a little carried away withthe salt. I hadn't even had time to blink when, behind me, I heard her voice warning me about the dangers to my health of a diet with too much salt. Ah! I forgot to say that Pepita, being a good person, has keys to my apartment (I don't remember when I gave them to her) so she comes and goes from my house whenever she pleases.

Lately I've been a little more worried, because I try to do everything well and in the right measure, to avoid my good neighbor Pepita giving me those scares she gives me by showing up like that, out of the blue. The thing is that I have realized that the more I worry about things, the more attention I pay to draw a straight and perfect line in my hair,the more I try to leave my shoes spotless..., has the immediate effect that Pepita is more time with me, the moreshe is for me, and the more she corrects me in everything I do.

The situation has reached an unsustainable point, we seem to have entered an endless spiral. The more I worry about doing things right so that she stops watching me and allows me to finally live-in peace, the more time she spends with me and the more and more demanding and unbearable my (in principle harmless) neighbor Pepita becomes.

Today I saw Pep, my neighbor in Quinto C. It had been a long time since we had talked. I don't know what he saw on my face, but the moment he looked at me he said, *"Mrs. Pepita, isn't it?* Barely out of breath, I asked him, "How do you know? *"Because Pepita, a long time ago, also had the keys to my* apartment and I can guess what you are going through. I immediately asked her, "And can she still enter your apartment whenever she wants? With a broad smile of satisfaction my neighbor in Fifth C, answers me - *"Well, no, because I got him to give me back the keys"*. Incredulous, I ask him again, "How did you do that? Now his smile is even wider, if that's possible. He crosses his arms and takes a breath as if he were preparing to make an endless speech: *"Look, at first it's complicated because you have to break yourroutines, you have to change your thought programs. Then it's a matter of always following the same new patterns you've learned:*

1) *Accept that she is there, and that the more force you use to push her away, the more she will cling to you.*

2) *If you notice his presence, try to pay him the minimum attention, do not give him importance, the more attention you give him the longer he will stay with you.Have you noticed that if you do not pay much attentionto him, he disappears immediately?*

3) *Learn to relativize. You are not going to die for not wearing your hair straight, just as you are not going to die because your heart is galloping for a while, or because you feel muscle tension, or because you feel sluggishness in your legs.*

4) *Look for distractions, things you can occupy your thoughts with, so you don't let her settle on the couch of your mind.*

I haven't heard from Pepita for some time now. At the beginning of putting my neighbor's recommendations into practice, on some occasions Pepita showed up unannounced,but as soon as she saw that I didn't pay much attention to her, she began to space out and shorten her visits. I think she stopped caring about me when I stopped caring about her.

I remember that the last time she visited me I was watching a movie when I began to feel a slight oppressive sensation in my chest, at the moment I began to listen to myself..., I felt her breathing. Pepita was next to me, worried, she told me that the sooner I went to the hospital the better... Then, I tried to remember the advice of my neighbor in Fifth C... I went back to focus on the movie... And, at the moment she was gone... She was gone!

Today, when I entered the living room, I saw a note next to some keys that I recognize. I picked it up with some nervousness, in fact for a moment I thought I felt a presence behind me, but I turned my attention to reading... It is a farewell note, where in a few lines you can read:

> *"I know that you no longer need me, little by little you have distanced yourself from me, you have stopped listening to me and paying attention to me. You no longer pay me the attention I deserve. For all this I have no choice but to abandon you and say goodbye, although for a while I will continue to watch you from a distance."*
>
> *Always yours:* **Pepita Anxiety**
> *PS. I give you back the keys to your life*

It is evident that people who suffer from anxiety, whether it isgeneralized or the result of a phobia, will not have enough to follow therecommendations of the neighbor of the Fifth C, I have not written this allegory with the intention of giving a remedy, or miracle cure, for anxiety, but I have written it with the intention that, whoever reads it knows more about the phenomenon about which this chapter is mostly about.

What is an irrefutable certainty is that **"If you don't pay attention to anxiety, it fades away"?** The problem is, **how do you do that?**

Perhaps it would be good (before answering the question in the previous paragraph) to describe how to perform a diagnostic evaluationof amaxophobia, as this is where we really should have started...

.

"Investing in knowledge produces
always the best benefits".
Benjamin Franklin [14]

Chapter 3

3 *How to make a diagnostic evaluation of amaxophobia*

In this chapter we make a complete exposition of how to conduct an interview related to the diagnostic evaluation of amaxophobia. In addition, to complete the diagnosis we pre-sent two questionnaires that assess amaxophobia, the first measuring primary amaxophobia (CEMIC 1) and the second (CEMIC 2) secondary amaxophobia.

3.1 The interview as an evaluation technique

Whatever the theoretical model on which the helping relationship is based, it is through the interview that the process of encounter or relationship between the professional expertin the assessment and treatment of phobias and the phobic person seeking help takes place. In order to enhance the personal development of the patient, or client (although many classifications of the interview have been made based on different criteria), in this case we will focus on the interview from the point of view of guidance and the helping relations-hip based on the theory of Carl Rogers[15].

The interview with Manel, in previous pages, follows the structural guidelines that we develop here in more detail.

---

[14] Benjamin Franklin: Born in Boston, USA, on 17/01/1706. He was a politician, scientist and inventor.

[15] Carl Rogers (1902 - 1987). Born in Illinois USA. Psychologist and promoter of the humanistic theory. His non-directive therapeutic model focuses onthe protagonism of the client.

3.2 Variables conditioning counseling and the helping relationship in the interview.

A. The orienting variable

The professional is the fundamental piece in the helping relationship. The success or failure in achieving the pro- posed objectives will depend on the characteristics of hisor her personality, his or her attitudes towards the personbeing counseled and his or her skills in facilitating communication. Thus, the basic competencies that everycounselor or therapist should possess to facilitate communication in the helping relationship are:

a. **Unconditional positive acceptance**: consists of allowing each individual to be different and at the same time unique, knowing that each person is a complex compendium of desires, thoughts and feelings of wide diversity.

b. **Empathic understanding**: this involves knowing howto put oneself in the other person's place, not only trying to grasp the objective meaning but also the subjective or personal meaning.

c. **Congruence**: the counselor must be congruent, sensible, sincere and authentic.

d. **Respect**: implies, on the part of the counselor, recognizing the other person's capacity to choose freely andthe right to make his or her own decisions.

e. **Responsibility**: in terms of the ability to ensure the client's independence, understood as encouragement from the counselor to the person being counseled, so that he/she takes the attitude of directing his/her ownlife. The client must accept responsibility for his or heractions and must be able to exercise his or her will, overand above the multitude of hesitations and tendencieshe or she may encounter.

In addition to the professional competencies described above,a set of specific skills that facilitate communication are important and necessary for the counselor, which are the following:

a. **Interlocutor-focused verbal skills:** knowing how toask the right questions, paraphrase, summarize and synthesize the sender's message.

b. **Verbal skills of influence and direction:** knowing how to analyze, interpret, share, confront, inform, summarize.

c. **Non-verbal skills:** knowing how to interpret gestures,postures, poses, changes in voice intonation, silences.

B. The variable oriented [16]

The oriented person is the protagonist who sets the rhythm and the plot of the situation. Their attitudes, skills, abilities and knowledge express the level of personal functioning andthe different levels of structuring-destructuring referred to two basic or fundamental cores:

a. Self-awareness of emotions, feelings, fears and desires. Here the helping relationship aims to provoke awareness, restructure the perception of these feelings and facilitate rational-emotional balance. This requires in the interviewee the capacity for self-exploration and self-discovery of those thoughts and feelings that maybe the genesis that provokes the behavior to be modified (in this case the phobic response).

b. Lack of training in decision making. People must have the habit of deciding and making their own personal decisions. The oriented person must know how to channel the facts and look for solutions to anticipate eventsand the reactions that arise from them. When the environment is perceived as hostile and threatening and thesubject does not find satisfactory answers, a response of thought inhibition may occur, where the person becomes paralyzed and tends to isolate him/herself.

In this case, the counselor's action is aimed at helping the client to review his or her way of seeing the context, to evaluate the new situation perceived, to reconstruct the facts or the experience based on the result of the previous evaluation and to seek, from there, strategies for action that will serve to make a decision that will provide an optimal response.

---

[16] We understand by oriented as the person who receives the orientation orassistance.

Interview models in amaxophobia

The classic outline for interview sequencing is:

1) Approach, 2) Exploration and 3) Conclusion. These phases are interrelated in such a way that sometimes it is not easy to determine precisely in which of them one is.

1) **Initial approach or moment:** in this phase the objectives of the interview are formulated, the situation is defined, expectations are made explicit, functions are structured and information is collected. It is the moment to create a welcoming atmosphere and to work on empathy.

2) **Exploration or central moment:** this phase constitutes the core of the interview, it goes deeper into the aspects identified in the previous phase, the most relevant ones are delimited, the reference model is expanded and, if necessary and possible, solutions are sketched out.

3) **Conclusion or final moment:** in this last phase, what was discussed is summarized, difficulties are clarified, if any, action strategies are proposed and decisions are made.

"Counseling as a helping relationship has many followers and has achieved great success applied to insecure, anxious, low self-concept, or behaviorally challenged subjects; it is an option that the counselor cannot ignore" (Rogers, 1972).

Without forgetting the points expressed in previous lines, here is a question guide that could be the common thread of the interview for the intervention in the phobia that we want to evaluate, know and treat. These questions should be asked in a relaxed setting and over the course of what could be construed as informal conversation. What we mean is that, although there is a formal structure and specific objectives (see previous lines), we must avoid: being too rigid, that is, not asking questions one after another, since this can give the interviewee the feeling that they are being subjected to an interrogation, if so, the interviewee can experience the situation as if it were an interrogation and not as a helping relationship.

In the following pages, we present two interviews designed specifically for the assessment of amaxophobia.

Sebastián Sánchez Marín

- The first (Interview 1) is aimed at people who, although they have never driven before, are afraid of driving. The typical typology of this client is the pre-driver who is postponing, consciously or unconsciously, obtaining his driving license because he is afraid to face driving.

- The second (Interview 2), is designed for people with previous driving experience and who have even been driving for years.

The result of the interview will provide us with the necessary information to determine our baseline and adjust the treatment, both in primary and secondary amaxophobia. *Interview 1. Assessment of primary amaxophobia*

For people who have no previous driving experience (have never driven a vehicle).

1. Why do you want to obtain a driver's license?

2. What do you think your theoretical learning will be like?

3. What do you think your hands-on learning will be like?

4. After obtaining your driver's license, do you think it will take you long to start driving?

5. Will you use the vehicle: daily, on weekends, from month to month...?

6. Can you tell me how long you have had the feeling of being afraid to drive?

7. Will you use the vehicle for: work, family, personal...?

8. The fear you feel about driving... do you think you will feel it whether you are driving alone or with someone else in the vehicle?

9. Do you remember if any stressful events happened in your life before the onset of your fear of driving?

10. When you began to feel fear of driving, what did you do to combat it?

11. What physical symptoms do you suffer when you startto feel fear invade you?

12. Did you explain your fear of driving to anyone?

13. Did you receive help from that someone?

14. Why do you think, you are afraid to drive?

15. When you decided to get your driver's license... did you do it gradually or was it radical?

16. Do you think you have made the right decision in deciding to start driving?

17. How do you feel about taking the step to drive?

18. Why have you decided to try it now, what is the reason?

19. Do you think anything has changed now to make you think you will be able to drive without fear?

20. How would you like to feel when you are driving?

Interview 2. Assessment of secondary amaxophobia

For people with previous driving experience.

1. What is your fear in driving?

2. How long have you been suffering from it?

3. Do you have any other fears?

4. What do you think is the cause of your fear of driving?

5. When you began to feel fear of driving, what did you do to fight it?

6. What do you think when you know you have to drive through a place, or a situation, that you are afraid of?

7. What physical symptoms do you suffer from when you start to feel fear creeping up on you?

8. Do you usually face these situations, even if you have a hard time, or on the contrary, do you avoid them or run away from them?

9. Who in your environment knows that you suffer from this fear?

10. Do you know any relaxation technique?

11. If yes, can you tell me which one?

12. Have you done meditation, visualization...?

13. Do you think it will be possible to overcome your phobia?

1.2 CEMIC Questionnaires 1 and 2

Undoubtedly, one of the indisputable instruments for obtaining information quickly and accurately is the questionnaire.
In our case we present the *"Driving Fear Evaluation Questionnaire" (*CEMIC). This instrument has been validated and tested with a sample of 336 pre-drivers, 166 of whom were male and 170 female. The analysis of the internal consistency of the primary amaxophobia scale by means of Cronbach's *alpha*coefficient corresponded to a value of 0.86, which is highly satisfactory (Sánchez 2011)[17].

The use of this instrument facilitates and enables us to categorize the levels of amaxophobia. In this way we can know whether we are dealing with a case of: absence of fear or low level, or medium or high fear of driving. To be more precise, the levels are established as follows:

- **Level 1:** No signs of amaxophobia. **Low Level**.

- **Level 2: Low-Medium Level** Amaxophobia.

- **Level 3: Medium Level** Amaxophobia.

- **Level 4: Medium-High Level** Amaxophobia.

- **Level 5: High Level** Amaxophobia.

Below, we present two questionnaires: the first is designed to be administered to people suffering from primary amaxophobia, while the second is specific to secondary amaxophobia.

---

[17] For more information see: S. Sánchez (2011). Validation of a brief ques- tionnaire for the assessment of fear of driving in pre-drivers. *Securitas VialisMagazine* 9, 33-48. (2011). Retrieved from https://www.infona.pl/re- source/bwmeta1.element.springer-99644a78-b77c-38bb-871b-438e8ca6d116

3.4.1 CEMIC Administration (1). Primary Amaxophobia

Specific questionnaire for the evaluation of primary amaxophobia **CEMIC (1) for pre-drivers**. Through this instrument we can know the level of amaxophobia suffered by the person who answers it. The interpretation of the results will facilitate the establishment of intervention criteria.

Specific Irrational Driving Fear Questionnaire (CEMIC (1) for pre-drivers)

1   I think I will be nervous when I have to drive.

1	2	3	4
Never	Somewhat	Quite often	Always

2.   I think if I had a choice, I would prefer someone else to drive.

1	2	3	4
Never	Somewhat	Quite often	Always

3.   I think driving will relax me.

1	2	3	4
Always	Quite a lot	A little	Never

4.   I think I will have the ability to drive.

1	2	3	4
A lot	Quite a lot	Very little	None

5.   If I think about driving, I feel muscle tension or discomfort.

1	2	3	4
Never	Somewhat	Quite often	Always

6.   It scares me to think that when I drive I might cause an accident.

1	2	3	4
Never	Somewhat	Quite often	Always

7.   When I carry passengers, I obsess about the fact that they think my driving is unsafe.

1	2	3	4
Never	Somewhat	Quite often	Always

8. The thought of going at a certain speed gives me a feeling of fear or vertigo.

1	2	3	4
Never	Somewhat	Quite often	Always

9. Obtaining a driver's license is more of an obligation than a pleasure.

1	2	3	4
Not true at all	Somewhat true	Fairly true	Absolutely True

10. I think I will be a clumsy driver.

1	2	3	4
Not true at all	Somewhat true	Fairly true	Absolutely True

11. I think the rest of the drivers will think of me as a nuisance.

1	2	3	4
Never	Somewhat	Quite often	Always

12. The thought of driving makes me insecure.

1	2	3	4
Never	Somewhat	Quite often	Always

13. I think that, even if I am cautious, others will collide with me.

1	2	3	4
Never	Somewhat	Quite often	Always

14. I think that when I have to drive it will generate a state of nerves.

1	2	3	4
Never	Somewhat	Quite often	Always

15. I think that when I drive, I will have to stop very often in order to calm down.

1	2	3	4
Never	Somewhat	Quite often	Always

3.4.2 CEMIC Administration (2). Secondary Amax-ophobia

Specific questionnaire for the evaluation of secondary amaxophobia **CEMIC (2) for drivers with driving experience.** Through this instrument we can know the level of amaxophobia suffered by the person who answers it. The interpretation of the results will facilitate the establishment of intervention criteria.

IMPORTANT: One of the observations to follow when passing this questionnaireis: Before administering the questionnaire, the person should be asked to answer the questionnaire by thinking about puttinghimself/herself in the situation of driving in the context of his/her fear.

Example: If you are afraid of driving on highways, you are told *"I would likeyou to answer this questionnaire with the thought that all the questions are associated with highway driving."*

Specific Questionnaire for Irrational Fear of Driving (CEMIC(2))

1. I get nervous if I know I have to drive.

1	2	3	4
Never	Somewhat	Quite often	Always

2. If I have a choice, I prefer someone else to drive.

1	2	3	4
Never	Somewhat	Quite often	Always

3. Driving relaxes me.

1	2	3	4
Always	Quite a lot	A little	Never

4. I think I have the ability to drive.A

1	2	3	4
A lot	Quite a lot	Very little	None

5. If I think about driving, I feel muscle tension or discomfort.

1	2	3	4
Never	Somewhat	Quite often	Always

6. It scares me to think that when I drive I can cause an acci-dent.

1	2	3	4
Never	Somewhat	Quite often	Always

7. If I am carrying passengers, I am obsessed with the fact thatthey think my driving is unsafe.

1	2	3	4
Never	Somewhat	Quite often	Always

8. Going at a certain speed gives me a feeling of fear or vertigo.

1	2	3	4
Never	Somewhat	Quite often	Always

9. Obtaining a driver's license was more out of obligation thanfor pleasure.

1	2	3	4
Not true at all	Somewhat true	Fairly true	Absolutely True

10. I am a dangerous driver.

1	2	3	4
Not true at all	Somewhat true	Fairly true	Absolutely True

11. I think the rest of the drivers think I'm a nuisance.

1	2	3	4
Never	Somewhat	Quite often	Always

12. Driving makes me insecure.

1	2	3	4
Never	Somewhat	Quite often	Always

13. I think that, even if I am cautious, others will collide with me.

1	2	3	4
Never	Somewhat	Quite often	Always

14. Driving will make me anxious or nervous.

1	2	3	4
Never	Somewhat	Quite often	Always

15. When I drive, I have to stop very often to calm down.

1	2	3	4
Never	Somewhat	Quite often	Always

QUESTIONNAIRE ANSWER SHEET (CEMIC)

	1	2	3	4
1.	☐	☐	☐	☐
2.	☐	☐	☐	☐
3.	☐	☐	☐	☐
4.	☐	☐	☐	☐
5.	☐	☐	☐	☐
6.	☐	☐	☐	☐
7.	☐	☐	☐	☐
8.	☐	☐	☐	☐
9.	☐	☐	☐	☐
10	☐	☐	☐	☐
11	☐	☐	☐	☐
12	☐	☐	☐	☐
13	☐	☐	☐	☐
14	☐	☐	☐	☐
15	☐	☐	☐	☐

Total:

Sebastián Sánchez Marín

CEMIC tabulation, example:

QUESTIONNAIRE ANSWER SHEET (CEMIC)

	1	2	3	4
1.	x			
2.		x		
3.		x		
4.	x			
5.			x	
6.				x
7.			x	
8.	x			
9.	x			
10				x
11		x		
12		x		
13				x
14			x	
15		x		

4 + 10 + 9 + 12

Total: 35

The crosses marked in the 1 column have a value equal to 1 (example 4 crosses = 4 points).
The crosses marked in the 2 column have a value equal to 2 (example 5 crosses = 10 points).
The crosses marked in the 3 column have a value equal to 3 (e.g. 3 crosses = 9 points).
The crosses marked in the 4 column have a value equal to 4 (example 3 crosses = 12 points).

3.4.3 CEMIC interpretation and intervention criteria (1 and 2)

The direct CEMIC score is used to indicate the degree of amaxophobia suffered by the pre-driver or driver and to focusassistance strategies according to the level of amaxophobia.

Level 1: Low level. Predominance of 1 (sum of scores between 15 and 25). No signs of amaxophobia.

Level 2: Low-Medium level Amaxophobia. Predominance of 1 and 2 (total score sum between 26 and 35): Symptoms ranging from the maximum of the Low level to the extreme minimum of the Medium level.

Level 3: Medium level Amaxophobia. Predominance of2 and 3 (total score sum between 36 and 39): Symptoms ranging from the maximum of the Low-Medium level(score close to 36) to the extreme minimum of the Medium-High level (score close to 39).

Level 4: Medium-High level Amaxophobia. Predominance of 3 and 4 (total score sum between 40 and 49): Symptoms ranging from the maximum of the medium level (score close to 40) to the extreme minimum of the high level (score close to 49).

Level 5: High level. Prevalence of 4 (total score sum between 50 and 60): Symptoms demonstrating a high level of amaxophobia. The more severe level is shown the closerthe score is to 60.

*"Those who are always back
of all are those who never
have gone nowhere".*
Antonio Machado [18]

Chapter 4

2 *Theoretical foundations of phobias*

It is difficult, as well as inaccurate and unprofessional, to argue about knowledge, interventions, or treatments without a theoretical basis. The theoretical foundation is what gives solidity and strength to any intervention program.

In this chapter we are going to specify some of the theoretical models that seem to us to be the most accurate and adequate for the knowledge and treatment of phobias or irrational fears.

You may find it tiresome to read about psychological models and theories that talk about behaviors and mental functioning. In addition, you may find it unnecessary in principle because you want to get to the point. In any case, this can be similar to when we buy a new generation cell phone, perhaps we do not read the instruction guide for use and operation, but it is always good to know where to find it in case we needto consult any section.

On the other hand, you will be able to see that, if not before, then later, throughout the course of this book we are going to talk about some of the theories that you will find in this chapter.

In my opinion, as I said in previous lines, the more information and knowledge you have about phobias, fears, anxiety, treatments, as well as psychological models and theories that have dealt with these issues... THE BETTER.

---

[18] Antonio Machado Ruiz (1875-1939). Spanish intellectual and poet.

4.5 Classical conditioning

At the beginning of the 20th century, a Soviet Union psycho-logist named Pavlov[19] noticed that, moments before feeding his dogs, without them having seen the food, they began to salivate. Perhaps, he thought that they had associated the time of day with the moment of eating and that is why they salivated before smelling or seeing it, or maybe not. It was then that he decided to set up an experiment in order to learn more about this type of response. For two weeks every day he changed the meal times and, always, a moment before putting the dish on the plate, he rang a bell. Naturally, for thefirst few days, the dogs only salivated when the food was in front of them. After that time, simply by ringing the bell (without the food being present) the dogs salivated profusely.Pavlov's dogs had associated a neutral stimulus (the sound ofthe bell) with a physiological response (salivation).

In fact, what Pavlov did was to establish and describe the func-tioning of the mechanisms of associationism[3]. Thesetheories have been evolving and deriving into more complexones, but which, even with some variation, are governed by the same principle of initial association. Pavlov called his model "classical conditioning". Today, Richard Bandler [20]and John Grinder[21], promoters of Neuro Linguistic Programming (PNL),call their model of association "anchoring".

An **anchor** is the automatic association between a stimulus and an emotional response. It consists of associating a sen-sory stimulus with an emotional state. The stimulus can be visual, auditory or kinesthetic. Generally, anchors are used to facilitate access to experiences stored in our memory in the form of positive or negative emotions. For an anchor to work,it is necessary: a) that it is associated with an experience; b)that the anchor is triggered at the moment of maximum sensation of that experience and; c) that the stimulus is always produced

---

[19] Ivan Petrovich Pavlov (1849 - 1936). He was born in Russia. He was a physiologist and psychologist. Nobel Prize in Physiology-Medicine in 1903.[3] According to the dictionary of Scientific and Psychological Psychology, associationism theories consider that a phe-nomenon can be explained from the association between elements more basic than the phenomenon itself, anassociation that the subject has previously experienced.

[20] Richard Bandler. Born in the USA, in 1950. Psychologist, mathematicianand computer scientist, co-founder, together with John Grinder, of Neuro Linguistic Programming (NLP).

[21] John Grinder. Born in the USA, in 1940. Psychologist and linguist, co-founder, to-gether with Richard Blander, of Neuro Linguistic Programming(NLP).

in the same context and with the same intensity.

In our daily life we go through a multitude of anchors that we use unconsciously. We hear a certain song and we remember when we listened to it in our teenage years and without kno- wing why it changes our mood. We pass in front of a toy store and the plastic smell of some toys takes us back to when we were children and we spent hours and hours playing and en- joying ourselves endlessly. Coffee, for many smokers, is a powerful anchor that makes them feel the urgent need to have a cigarette just by smelling it.

The bad news is that many fears are reinforced by negative anchors.

> Remember the story of Manel's amaxophobia and the trick his unconscious played on him by associating (anchoring), driving through a tunnel with his fear of losing control of his vehicle, with his anxietysymp- toms. This anchoring is responsible for the factthat, from then on, every time Manel drives througha tun- nel he goes into a state of panic, so this wouldbe a good example of negative anchoring.

The good news is that we can counteract a negative anchor with a positive one, i.e., in the same way that a stimulus has been associated with a negative emotion, we can associate an- other stimulus with a positive emotion and bring it up so that the positive emotion neutralizes the negative one and also the symptoms that accompany it (we will see how later).

On the previous page I commented on how a conceptual evo- lution had been taking place from associationism, through classical conditioning, to what in PNL is known as anchoring. We have also seen that anchoring refers to the association be- tween a stimulus and an emotion. This circumstance ex- plains many of the issues that we will be unpacking little by little throughout this text.

From my point of view, the role of emotions is a fundamental asset not only in the treatment of phobias, but with everything that has to do with our balance and mental health.

It is for this reason that I consider important to include in this chapter a section on emotions.

Likewise, it is clear that not everything in us are emotions. In fact, we could say that in our brain there are (albeit in a metaphorical sense) two perfectly differentiated rooms: one of them houses the emotions and the other shelters reason. Let us first enter into the dependencies of the latter.

4.6 Stay of reason

Human beings have the ability to make sense of everything that surrounds us, to interpret and give meaning to the events that surround us through cognition. Cognition could be defined as the processing of information, based on the perception that comes from our senses, and its subsequent elaboration when merged with our beliefs, values, expectations, our knowledge stored in our memory and with the learning accumulated through experience.

Taking into account what was expressed in the previous paragraph, it could be said that reason is what makes possible our capacity to think, to make decisions, to opt and choose among answers that satisfy us in the resolution of problems.

> When Manel's **reason**, full of logic and coherence, could not find a rational explanation to justify his symptoms of muscular tension and tightness in his chest, at the moment he was going through a tunnel,it was when his reason gave way to an exacerbated panic, because no matter how hard his reason searched, he could not find any danger as a real cause that would satisfy his uncertainty.

4.7 Stay of emotions

It would be unthinkable to talk about fear without mentioning emotions, since fear is one of the basic emotions, along with joy, anger and sadness. Being so, and following the idea of documenting everything that has to do with fear, whether irrational or not, let's go a little deeper into this area...

An emotion is an involuntary reaction to an event that affects our expectations and plans. When this reaction is produced before a stimulus whose intensity affects our protection system, without any affective meaning, we are talking about a reflex, for example, when we move our hand away from a stove when we notice that we are burning, or when we give an automated response, such as answering that two plus twois four.

To arrive at the distinction of emotion we have to rely on two conditions:

a) The first condition is that the response, at first, is auto-matic and universal, that is to say, that it arises without thinking and can be interpreted by any human being. Thus, the reaction of pressing hard on the steering wheeland stepping on the brake, when exiting a curve due to speed-ing, is a reaction provoked by the emotion of fear ofgetting hurt or losing one's life.

b) The second condition is that the emotion itself is recogni-zable through non-verbal language. Cicero[22] said that *"The face is the mirror of the soul"*, and that is because it is very difficult for emotions not to be reflected in our corporal ex-pression, especially in our countenance. Mimes know this very well, as they do not need to say a word forus to know if they are sad, happy, angry, terrified or sim-ply surprised.

It is rare that an object, person or situation generates only one emotion, unless it is a very extreme situation. On the other hand, there are events that, by their very nature, suchas a pleasant surprise, generate several emotions at the sametime. This circumstance allows us a very rich and complex emotional life, which explains why we value art, literature, music, po-etry...

For many years emotions have been studied as a separate en-tity from our behavior, as something irrational and primarythat responded to instincts. Nowadays, it has been shown that emotions are closely related to learning processes and that, together with reason, they interact in the construction of the subjective reality of each person. When reason and emotions go in the same direction, psychological congruence, well-being and satisfaction are obtained; when there is a discrepancy be-tween reason and emotion, an internal conflict ofdifficult solu-tion is produced if the situation is not redirected towards a state of equilibrium between the two (Festinger[23], 1957).

If we are afraid of needles, why do we suffer from this phobia and our doctor has told us that it is essential that we have a blood test, we enter into a cognitive dissonance, because our emotional mind (our fear) is telling us *"not to talk about it"*, while our reason is screaming for us to follow the treatment.

---

[22] Marcus Tullius Cicero (106 - 43 B.C.). Consul of Rome. Writer, Jurist,Orator and Poli-tician.

[23] Leon Festinger (1919 - 1989). He was born in New York. He was a professor of Social Psychology and author of the Theory of Cognitive Dissonance.

The problem is that, in this case, no matter what we do, we will feel dissatisfied if we have not managed to converge thought and emotion towards a common purpose. If we decide to undergo the treatment (being pricked with a needle) we will be overcome by fear, and the anxiety mechanism will unfailingly start up and, if we avoid the fear (not exposing ourselves to the phobic situation), we will lapidate our capacity to be free in our decision making. Paradoxically, fear will have dominated our decisions and we will feeltrapped by it.

Of course, the effort to make emotions and thoughts work in the same direction will be proportional to the consequences that we can obtain in the normal performance of our life. The level of effort to overcome fears, in this particular case fear of needles, will not be the same in a person who has never been sick and does not even remember where the ambulatoryof his town is located; than a person with serious health problems and therefore is always surrounded by medical personnel, needles and medicines.

An example of an intervention to align reason and emotion in the same direction, in order to facilitate the therapeutic process, is summarized in the following episode, where a part of one of the initial sessions in an agoraphobia treatment is described:

Miriam panics about driving at night

Miriam. First part

> Miriam is 39 years old, married and has two young children. She has been a daily driver for 15 years. The initial interview and the score of 52 on the CE-MIC 2 questionnaire confirm that Miriam is a case of High Level amaxophobia (Level 5).
>
> During the conversation he tells us that he has been driving for years without any problem, and without any limitation, because it was the same for him to drive in the city as on the road, or on highways or freeways, at night or during the day....
>
> She also tells us that, in her opinion, it all started about three years ago, the night she was taking her 18-month-old son to the emergency room of the County Hospital. Pol, her baby, had been unusually

quiet and listless that morning. The thermometer reading only confirmed her suspicion that something was wrong. During the afternoon Pol'sfever continued to rise, and at 7 p.m. (already darkin winter), seeing Pol's fever, he was still in a stateof high fever. (already dark in winter), seeing that the thermometer was still accumulating tenths, shedecided not to wait any longer and took her son to the emergency room.

The trip to the hospital was well known to Miriam, as she had already made a few trips when her husband Ferrán had a motorcycle accident and was hospitalized for three long months to recover from the polytraumas suffered in his left leg.

While she was fastening the seat belts of Pol's car seat, she began to feel a little nervous, as if she was having difficulty breathing, the buckle was reluctant to click into place and the lack of light didn't help either... She thought that the uncomfortable position could also be the cause of her shortness of breath...

With the car back on track, on the road that would take her to the Hospital, she began to realize that she had promised her boss that, first thing tomorrow morning, she would deliver the report of a new project that had been entrusted to her... How was she going to finish the report, if instead of being at the computer she was driving to the Hospital, with her 18-month-old baby? The worst thing was not how she could finish the report on time but being in the uncertainty of what could happen to her littleone. She hoped it was nothing, but... You never know!

It is barely two kilometers to go and Miriam is startled... Her breathing is short, it seems that not enough air is reaching her lungs... She forces her breath and accelerates the rhythm of the air inhalations... Suddenly, she thinks that from one moment to the next she is going to suffer a sudden death due to lack of air. She is even more terrified to realize that her baby is with her and that, if she diesfrom running out of breath, the car will crash with her little one in it.

Just when he thinks the worst is about to happen, he

begins to notice that his breathing has stopped being so irregular... The lights of the Hospital havecaught his attention and, he doesn't know why, butit has been like a miraculous balm that has put everything in its place.

Between one thing and another she spent two hours in the emergency room of the hospital. Now she is calm, Pol's ear infection has been diagnosed and the treatment has started to take effect. The doctor on duty has told her not to worry, to follow the indicated antibiotic treatment dosage, and that in a few days her little one will be fighting as usual.

Now she is well, her baby is better and she is still in time to have dinner with her partner, who is home from work, and she will even be able to finish the report that will promote her in the company without any problem. You could say that, at this moment, she is happy.

The limp sound of the old diesel engine of his rickety Ford Fiesta breaks the silence of the Hospital's parking lot. Everything is going well. Miriam joins the road and has barely gone a few kilometers when she notices that she abruptly runs out of air. She tries to remedy the situation, breathing in a hurried manner, and feels her heart racing for seconds. The feeling of imminent death returns... She desperately looks for a place to move her vehicle away from the road...

In less than a minute Miriam is stopped, off the road, in a space provided for the entrance of an industrial building, which at this hour is closed. She calls her husband Ferrán and tells him to come andpick her up, that she is very nervous, that there wasa moment when she thought she was going to die and that she doesn't dare to move the car from where she is...

From that moment on she has never been able to drive normally during the night, she remembers that at first, she had thought of using a paper bag, because she had read on the Internet that the symptoms she suffered from were similar to "Hyperventilation Syndrome" and in the movies, especially in the United States, people used the remedy of breathing through a paper bag to regulate breathing. The problem (Miriam kept saying) is *"How are you going to drive around with one hand on the steering wheel, the other holding a bag, while your face is stuck in the damn paper bag?"* As she was telling me all this, in Miriam's face, you could see the anguish and despair. *"You have to help me, Doctor, I don't want to die from lack of air, especially not while driving"*.

I can still easily see his face of disbelief when I told him that it must be very hard to think that you can die of asphyxiation just for carrying out such a common activity as driving at night. Even harder, if possible, to think that this can happen when you are driving a vehicle that, due to its movement and weight, accumulates a large amount of kinetic energy, so you can hurt yourself and others...Only..., the circumstance you fear so much (dying of asphyxiation when driving at night) is more thanunlikely to happen.

*"What do you mean? "*I mean that, in a respiratory failure caused by an anxiety crisis, it would be quite complicated for someone to die, of course: although we can vary our breathing voluntarily, our central nervous system, specifically the medulla oblongata,is responsible for maintaining, automatically, the frequency and rhythm of breathing ... You will agreewith me that we do not usually think, or be continuously aware of whether we breathe or not, or ...,if we do it faster or deeper sometimes than others,is that so?"

"The problem occurs when, for whatever reason (in this case anxiety) we consciously interfere in the automated functioning of our spinal cord, which, as we said before, is responsible for maintaining adequate breathing and adapted to the oxygen demand of our body: slowed breathing if we are at rest and somewhat faster if we increase our rate of movement, for example, running or accelerate the pace because we miss the bus".

"The point, and without going into minute details, is that breathing seeks homeostasis (balance) between the oxygen we breathe in and the carbon dioxide we exhale. This function should not worry us because, as I mentioned before, the respiratory center of our medulla oblongata is there to take careof it and it does it, autonomously and unconsciously,without mistakes or errors. The problem arises when someone, for whatever reason, decides to interfere in this efficient and automatic functioning ofbreathing. In your case, when you notice the first signs of shortness of breath, you decide to take control by breathing faster, without realizing that the faster you breathe, the more you unbalance the in-flow and out-flow of oxygen and carbon dioxide. Thisimbalance triggers all the alarms, the sensation of suffocation is greater, so you breathe faster. And so, you end up in a never-ending loop".

Miriam looks at me with an ironic face and says, *"It's just that I have such a bad time, I get so sick that I feel like I'm dying and that's when I get out of control.*

I look at Miriam and say, "Do you realize that all your fears converge in the fact that you may die of asphyxiation? *"Yes, it seems so,"* she replies, "Well,let me continue my demonstration that this is unlikely to happen, because there seems to be a step in this whole process (driving at night, having an anxiety attack, hyperventilating and dying) that you have skipped.
"I don't understand. What step have I skipped?" -
"Well, perhaps the most important one, of course, is that, although it is true that, in a process of hyperventilation, the person may feel dizzy, with weakness in the legs, and even, in the worst of circumstances, it is possible that he may faint..., in these cases it is unlikely, not to say impossible, thathe may die due to lack of air".

Miriam looks at me expectantly, as if waiting for me to confirm what she seems to have already understood, and before I can continue my rant, she says....
"I can see it now, it is unlikely that I could die from lack of air, because before I die, I would first start to feel dizzy, then I would pass out, and once I have lost consciousness, I would again leave the control in the hands of the autonomic nervous system specialized in breathing, and therefore I would return to normal breathing."

> We both express our complicity with a smile as I tell him... - "Well, that's it!"

It would be absurd if I wanted you to believe that Miriam's treatment culminated here, because, besides not being true, I would be underestimating your intelligence and your unflappable patience that has read me up to this point. What I can assure you is that all this information and knowledge, which Miriam integrated that day, facilitated her treatment and therefore changed her way of seeing and facing her phobia.

You may be wondering why she suffered the crisis the day she was taking her son Pol to the hospital and not when she was taking her husband Ferrán, because surely some of the trips she made, taking her husband, were also at night.

The answer is simple and, even at the risk that sometimes it can get complicated, surely (because of what we have explained in Manel's story) you already have it.

At the time when Miriam was making the night journey to the hospital with her young son Pol, Miriam was overwhelmed with stress and anxiety. When this happens, there is a moment when anxiety manifests itself through physiological symptoms (chest pain, accelerated heart rate, paresthesia in the hands and/or feet, difficulty in breathing, etc., etc.). This manifest explosion of anxiety happened at the very moment when Miriam was driving at night and her mind did what the human mind does best ASSOCIATE (anchor) her anxiety symptoms with night driving. If that manifestation of anxiety symptoms had happened when she was traveling on a train, or inside an elevator (...), from then on Miriam would feel anxiety every time she got on a train, or used an elevator, so she would have ended up developing a phobia of trains, or elevators, or whatever else she had associated with her anxiety. In this case, the association has been established by Classical Conditioning (more on this later). Night driving has been associated with the hyperventilation response.

As we have said before, one of the responses associated with anxiety, in addition to the physiological symptoms, and the avoidance or flight from the phobic stimulus, is the cognitive response, where our ideas, thoughts and beliefs fill us with worries and fears. And, thinking that fear is a basic emotion, perhaps it is time for us to enter the realm of emotions.

4.8 Managing emotions

Albert Ellis[24], one of the precursors of the cognitive behavioral psychology current, defended that <u>thoughts are the basis of emotions</u>, although this statement is the starting point of Rational Emotive Therapy (RET), has its origin in a phrase written, approximately one hundred years before Christ was born, by Epictetus of Phrygia[25]who said:

> *"It's not the things that happen that disturbyou, it's the opinion you have of them."*

Let's see how Epictetus would do, today, to explain why a person who has become unemployed ends up showing de-

pression: if someone becomes unemployed (*things that happen*) and manifests sadness (*disturbance*) he is not sad because he is unemployed (*things that happen*), but because of all the thoughts (*opinion*) that have been going through his head.

Let us distinguish why: If after losing your job you have thoughts such as: *"With my age it will be impossible to find another job; surely, if I cannot pay the mortgage my family and I will find ourselves in the street; my God, I will have to beg; I will lose all my friends; these things only happen to me; I am a poor wretch..."* Do all these thoughts seem to youenough to generate and feed the emotion of sadness and eventually end up in depression?

If, on the other hand -the same person, in the same circumstances-, after losing his job he has thoughts like: *"It is true that I have lost my job, but it is also true that my unemployment insurance will allow me to be calm for a good season; this is a great time for family ties to become stronger; now that my economic position will not be so buoyant I may lose some friends, but the real ones will always be with me; as I will have enough free time I will take up again the idea of the small business that I have always thought could work...".* Do you think that with these thoughts the result will also be sadness? In this case, the person will probably not be overflowing with joy, but he will not be sad either, because he has managed to neutralize his emotional discomfort by controlling his thoughts.

---

[24] Albert Ellis (1913-2007). He was a pioneer in cognitive therapy (1955). One of his best known books is "Rational Emotive Therapy", published in2005 by Pax de Mexico.
[25] Epictetus of Phrygia (55-135). Greek philosopher. Stoic school

Ellis developed this theory and turned it into a model of help and guidance known as Rational Emotive Therapy (RE), whichis currently followed by many Cognitive-Behavioral psychologists.

4.9 Tell me what you think and I will tell you what you feel

Rational Emotive Therapy (RE) is based on the hypothesis that the cause of psychological distress arises from illogical, irrational or unrealistic thinking: Albert Ellis summarized his model of psychological intervention with the following words:

> "... If individuals suffer emotional disorders because they accept, without thinking, certain illogical premises, there is reason to believe that they can be persuaded or somehow taught to think more logically and rationally and, therefore,to curb their own disorders."

Although it is true that Ellis uses the term emotion in his writings, we are going to talk about feelings. The reason is that,if we stick to the definitions previously expressed in this book,an emotion would be difficult to manage (remember that it arises automatically and unconsciously), while the feeling - being the sum of an emotion plus the thoughts that are generated since we are aware of the emotion- could be manageable through the control of thoughts, that is, if you manageto take charge of your thoughts, starting by being aware of them, then you can also manage them. In this way, it is possible to change the initial feeling. This being so, we consider it more appropriate to speak in terms of "feelings" and not "emotions".

Let us see, with an example, how from the perspective of Ellis' ERT (with the incorporation of some modifications of our own) feelings can be managed. To do so, we will continue with Miriam's story.

Miriam: second part

> Ever since the episode in which Ferrán had to rescue her from her first anxiety attack in the face of her night driving, Miriam had been cheating on any moment that had to do with driving at night. She had become an expert in avoiding or running away from situations where she suspected that she might have

to drive and suffer an attack.

In this case, as in many others, the problem reaches its extreme when you run out of options. Until now, the alternatives had been working: Ferrán drove at night and, if it was not feasible, she organized herself to always move around under the protection of sunlight. In fact, if it were not for the news, she had just been given, she could have continued with these routines until the end of her days, but some-times chance or fate plays a trick on us.

Miriam has just been notified that next year she will be the Accounting Manager and that means more responsibility (she doesn't mind), more money (sheis delighted), and..., rotating shifts... Horror! That means that during the winter months she will haveto drive at night to get to the department she will be managing on time. And this is where your head won't stop spinning. Her thinking (cognitive response) will not leave her alone (run - run - run - run - run). But she has time (she thinks), *"There is still almost a year to go before Martin retires and I take over his position... "Maybe it would be good if I told Ferran that we should start making night driving incursions..."*

The ringing of the telephone brings her out of her reverie, the expression on her face reflects in an instant her concern... Her boss has just informed her that tomorrow the delegate from Europe is arriving at El Prat airport for an urgent meeting. He tellsher that he has to prepare the meeting in the office,and that the most operative and efficient way is forher to be at the airport at 6:30 a.m. to pick him upwhen he arrives for his flight from Amsterdam.

Miriam begins to hyperventilate while an imaginary (for her real) slab is pressing on her thorax. Her imagination (cognitive response) gives her no respite. She feels terrible. The colleagues who witnessthe situation, believing that Miriam is suffering a heart attack, call 112 and in less than 30 minutes Miriam is being treated in the emergency room for possible heart failure...

The next day at 10:30 a.m. a cab takes her back

home. Diagnosis: "Anxiety Crisis". Rescue treatment: "Diazepam: Prescription: Follow a combined procedure of pharmacology and psychology.

At this point in Miriam's story, I propose to analyze, from a Cognitive-Behavioral perspective, specifically from ERT, how Miriam will strengthen through this run - run thinking, the

initial association between driving at night and the anxiety crisis experienced at the time she took her baby to the ER, tothe point of turning it into a real case of amaxophobia or fearof driving.

4.10 The intervention process

The help, from the rational emotive model, consists of replacing inappropriate thoughts and beliefs with adaptive and rational beliefs. The main method is known as **Thought Debate** and is basically an adaptation of the scientific method to everyday life. That is, if our thoughts are mainly responsible for our negative and inappropriate feelings, we can feel better if we learn to think by means of a scientific method according to which such beliefs could be considered as hypotheses, so their validity or invalidity has to be determined be-fore being accepted or rejected. The steps to be followed arethe following:

Discover the beliefs that are at the root of the problems and see clearly that they are illogical, unrealistic, and that they are the cause of our discomfort.

Learn to debate those beliefs in order to demonstrate to yourself how and why they are not logical or rational.

Discriminate irrational and non-constructive beliefs from rational and constructive ones, showing how the latter lead to better results. Change irrational beliefs for more rational and logical beliefs.

For each of these beliefs, one has to look for why they are irrational. For example: the belief that an individual must have universal love and acceptance is irrational because it isarbitrary and because, invariably, it will produce discomfort, frustration and disappointment, since it is impossible for everyone to like you and for everyone to love you; there will always be someone who dislikes you. Similarly, it is irrationalto define our value as human beings by merits or material achievements, properties obtained..., since the value of a person cannot be measured in numerical terms. What price would you put on your partner, your children, or your parents, or siblings? 1.000€, 10.000€..., one million, three cars, two doctorates? People are loved for what they are and not for what they have. Therefore, it is illogical to think that my life-long friends now love me more because I have finished my Master's degree, or because I drive a Ferrari, or because I wear Armani suits. I think that real friends will love you just the same, even if you wear jeans from the flea market, and if they don't, it would be better to look for new friendships, don't you think?

Another important characteristic of these beliefs is that they are based on **"MUST"**, **"MUST HAVE"**, **"SHOULD"** impositions. A basic tenet of the rational emotive model is that absolutist impositions such as ("**you should** behave this way","**I must** be a nice person in all circumstances", etc.), createcognitive distortions that lead to conflict and psychological distress.

The **Debate of thought** is based on the A-B-C-D-E paradigm (plus F), where we find a structured series of listed phases. To these five phases we have added one more (F) so that atthe end of the process a reflection is made on the lessons learned from the analysis of the experience following all the phases of the **A-B-C-D-E-F** process.

The intervention protocol that we are now briefly presenting will be further developed focusing on Miriam's story, described above.

A. Activating experience:

Search for the apparent cause that has provoked the feeling of discomfort.

B. Thoughts and beliefs:

Examine what thoughts and self-verbalizations are going through our mind after A (A. Activating experience) has occurred.

C. Consequences of thoughts:

Analyze what feelings and behaviors are occurring as a cause of B.

D. Discussion of thoughts:

Transform irrational, illogical or false thoughts and/or beliefs into more coherent and rational, more real ideas involving debates, logical challenges, calculation of probabilities about those thoughts.

E. Final result:

Check how we feel, what our emotional state is, after having properly confronted irrational ideas and beliefs with our rational and logical thoughts.

F. Learning from experience:

In order to internalize what we have learned: Perform a visualization exercise on the lessons we have learned from the experience. This visualization will help to forge new mental programs, or patterns of behavior, that will facilitate the emotional adaptation to future similar situations.

4.11 Applying the A-B-C-C-D-E-F paradigm to Miriam's case

A. Activating experience:

Miriam is told that tomorrow morning at 6:30 a.m. shehas to be at El Prat airport to pick up the delegate fromEurope. This means that she has to drive at night and take someone important in the chain of command of the multinational company where she works.

B. Thoughts and beliefs:

The illogical, or irrational, thoughts that run through Miriam's mind are: P1 *"When the Delegate sees how nervous I get driving he's going to think I'm useless"* ;P2 *"I'm a failure in every way"*; P3 *"These things only happen to me"*; P4. *"I will never get over this phobia"*.These unrealistic thoughts give way to....

C.   Consequences of thoughts:

The emotions and feelings that Miriam feels are a pro- duct of the illogical thoughts of phase B. You will agree with me that with those thoughts you can only expect that, after a while, she will feel sad and depressed (her and anyone else), so it further reinforces her idea that: the best thing she can do is forget about being the head of the Accounting Department, as she is a failure and will never overcome this absurd fear. What to do with those thoughts?

D.   Discussion of thoughts:

In this phase we seek to change the thoughts of phase B for more realistic and logical ones, for more positive ones. The purpose is that, by modifying our thoughts (ideas and beliefs) we also modify our feelings, our emotions.

Let's see how: Once we become aware that those thoughts are negative, illogical or irrational (we search our mind for what thoughts are going on at that moment) we will chip away at them in order to turn them around and move them from neg- ative to more neutral thoughts... In the end, we will feel better. Let's see how:

1.   Negative thought P1: *"When the Delegate sees hownerv- ous I get driving he will think I am useless"*. Itis possible that the Delegate, if he sees her hyper- ventilating, might think that there is something wrong with her, he might even think that she is use- less at driving, but Miriam should realize that she was not hired for her driving skills, but for her skillsas an accountant, for being a responsible person and very committed to her job.

   • Negative thought P2: *"I am a failure in every way"*.
     − Faced with this thought Miriam should ask herself:

       ▪ What if we were to take a look at other aspects of Miriam's life... The questions she should ask her- self to debate this thought are: Are you a failure as a mother? And as a wife? What would your friends say about you? And by the way, how is it that, out of 6 colleagues in your department at promotion level, for the position of accounting manager, you have been chosen...? We could go on, but I don't think we need to argue any further to see that this thinking is absurd and illogical.

- As for the thought; P3 *"These things only happen to me".* It would be nice if Miriam could prove that phobias and anxiety do not discriminate, nor do they care if you are tall or short, beautiful or ugly, skinny or thick, rich or poor, blonde or brune- tte Suffering or not suffering from a phobia has more to do with your way of perceiving and fee- ling the reality that surrounds you than with being a win- ner or a failure, as an example we only have to think of famous artists who have triumphed and, at a certain point in their career, have had to take a break because they suffered from stage fright. I am thinking of Pastora Soler, or the in- combus- tible Joaquín Sabina, both have fought against their phobic situation, have recovered, and today they are still going strong on stage.

  The problem is greatly aggravated if we allow our- selves to be carried away by victimhood and per- ceive everything as great misfortunes that only happen to us. Montaigne[26] in a single sentence concretizes the idea I am sharing with you: *"My life has been full of terrible misfortunes, mostof which never happened".* How right this French philoso- pher was, because too many times we anchor our- selves in a state of infinity because we fill our heads with worries about things that have never happened or that will happen. Negative thought P4: *"I will never overcome thisphobia".*

- Continuing with the technique of discussing the negative, catastrophic and irrational thoughtsthat go through Miriam's mind, perhaps it would be good for her to implement an exercise similarto the following (as we have done in P1, P2 and P3):

- Later on we will see the importance that the useof terms such as: never, never, always, always, only, only, only have for our internal language (what we say to ourselves). In principle, the useof such a rigid term hinders our ability to change,it is too

---

[26] Michel Eyquem de Montaigne (1533 - 1592). France: philosopher, humanist, politician and writer of the Renaissance.

extreme a word, it is difficult to maintain the "never", for example "I will never look at that person again", "I will never fall in love again" ... **Everything comes and everything passes, no matter how much we insist on the contrary.**

- In this case Miriam only has to look at the statistics to see that the percentage of people who have suffered from a phobia and have been completely cured, or have managed to reduce their symptoms to a level that is not disabling, is high and satisfactory. Thus, I could confirm that there are many more people who have overcome this disorder than those who continue to suffer from it. Perhaps it would be good for her to start for- getting that absolutist message *"I will never over-come this phobia"*, because if others have achieved it, she can also achieve it. Knowing statistical data can be useful to know that: we are not a unique case and that there is a very high percentage of people who have overcome it.

Sensible people think in probabilities, those who are not so sensible believe in chance *"Let's see if I get lucky and get cured".* Or they think that what happens to them is because it is written in their destiny, or it is a punishment from God. I am not going to discuss these questions here, since I have already dealt with this subject in the book **"You decide, you change, you live"**. But, be that as it may, and in the meantime, it would not be superfluous for Miriam to make an effort and keep adding positive thoughts of the type:

- *"Well, it's true that this is a bummer, but it's also one more of the many obstacles that one encounters on the road of life. I don't think that the people who really love me, like my family, or my friends are going to stop because I get more or less nervous driving, just as I don't think my colleagues and bosses are going to give less value to my work because of this." "Besides, if other people have managed to overcome this problem, I can too. I have achieved other things that a priori I thought would be unattainable"... "Go ahead, I can!".*

It is easy to realize that, if we can make these the new thoughts that occupy Miriam's mind, surely the path towards demotivation and sadness will have been stopped And, through the Thought Debate (D), the way has been given to revert her feelings, thus achieving that Miriam's distress and bad feeling are transformed into more neutral and bearable feelings of peace, calm and confidence, which are what this protagonist needs to begin to weave the net that will help her to escape from her psychic imprisonment.

At the end of this phase, Miriam should "reframe"[27] the situation and program new objectives that fit her new reality, which is none other than to accept that she is in a situation that will be easier to get out of with the help of her family, friends, colleagues, and perhaps a professional who can helpher find her way in a guided and safe manner.

E.   Final result:

Check how, after having discussed the thoughts in phase "D", the level of uneasiness and sadness has de- creased. It may be interesting to have elaborated in phase "C" (consequences of thoughts) a scale from 1 to 10, where 1 would correspond to the absence of dis- tress and 10 to maximum distress, with the intention of scoring ourselves in phase "C" and re-recording scores at the end of phase "D". In this way we could verify if after the procedure we have managed to lower the score on the scale, in this case, of discomfort and discouragement.

Thus, in most cases it is found that, after the Thought Debate (phase D), the score has decreased sufficientlyfor the person to move away from the feeling of dis- comfort and end up relativizing what is happening to him/her.

Things are not always the way you want them to be andthat does not mean that the world ends, or that it is catastrophic or terrifying, on the contrary, generally nothing happens and the proof is that, when some timehas passed of events where we have had a bad time, possibly we do not even remember them. Hence the idea that we are only affected by what we

---

[27] Reframing in Neuro Linguistic Programming (NLP) is a technique that allows us to perceive situations according to different perspectives. Adapt the behavior or emotion to the new situation. An analogy, from photography, would be: If you approach or move away from the object you want to photograph you must, in order to obtain a good image, "reframe" the cameralens again. If you do not do this, the view of the object will be out of focus.

want to be affected (Epictetus of Phrygia).

F.   Learning from experience:

In order that the learning extracted from the experience rein-forces the structure of our new way of managing our feelings, it would be an excellent idea that, at the end of the day, an exercise of visualizing what happened is carried out, reviewing the whole process from phase "A" to "E". How we have been aware of the activating experience (A), how we have "hunted" the negative thoughts (B), how those negative thoughts have generated, in this case, the feeling of sadness (C), how the thought debate (D) has transformed the negative ideas into neutral or positive thoughts, and how, at the end, we can see that the result (E) confirms that our level of discomfort has decreased.

All these steps will be reinforced if we vivify, through visuali-zation[28] in phase "F", all the experience that hascaused us that discomfort (later we will develop the technique of visualization by imagination, do not worry).By the way, the exercise of re-viewing at the end of theday the experiences that have oc-curred, in order to learn from them, is only advisable if what has happened has stirred our feelings and we have been able to neutralize them. If this is not the case, it is not a good idea to occupy our heads with worries, absurd or not, just before going to sleep.

At first, following this method to manage your emotions and feelings may seem complex, but if there is something I have learned, throughout my personal and professional expe-rience, is that there is nothing that cannot be achieved if we are able to put in a little effort, patience and a lot of perse-verance. There is a phrase from Henry Ford[29] that summa-rizes very well, in my opinion, this thought... *"Whether you think you can, or think you can't, you are right".*

In your case:

---

[28] Visualization is a technique that consists of visualizing past situations, orimagining fu-ture situations. It has to be practiced in a place where we can enjoy a quiet time, where we can concentrate on what we want to visualizeor imagine. It is generally done with closed eyes and in a comfortable position that allows our body to relax.
[29] Henry Ford (1863 - 1947). American. Inventor. Founder of the Ford Mo-tor Company. Promoter of the first automobile (Ford T) produced in chain

- Are you one of those who generally think you can?

- Do you believe in yourself? O...

Are you one of those who think that it is up to others to decide whether or not you are worthy of achieving what you set out to do?

A little more about the Rational Emotive model

One of the common problems with phobias is anticipation. To anticipate means to deal with something before it happens (pre-worry). The person suffering from a phobia begins to suffer long before facing the phobic stimulus because of his or her pre-worry. In Miriam's case, it is clear that it was worry, after learning that she had to drive at night the next day in order to bring her company's delegate from the airportto the headquarters, that triggered her anxiety episode and landed her in the hospital. By the way, the fact that she washospitalized because of this crisis, unconsciously "avoiding" going to look for the delegate, or in other words, escaping from the phobic situation by not facing it, made her fear andher anxiety responses grow even more, since anxiety feeds on fears and fears feed on anxiety.

4.11.1 Control of worries and thoughts inphobias

Did you know that every day we have about 60,000 thoughts? And what, approximately 80% of these thoughts are the same as the previous day. Undoubtedly, we are continuously thinking, our brain does not rest, even in too many occasionswe are not even aware of our thoughts, that is because we do not pay enough attention to it, the difficult thing is not tothink about anything. It seems as if we should always have something to occupy or worry our minds. It is also true that if we make an effort, we can observe our thoughts, reflect on them and try to modify them so that they produce well-being. Marcus Aurelius[30] said that "The happiness of your life depends on the quality of your thoughts". In the same line, Buddha[31] warned us that "Your worst enemy cannot harm you as much as your own

---

[30] Marcus Aurelius Antonius Augustus (121 - 180). Roman emperor. He was nick-named the Wise.
[31] *"Everything we are is the result of what we have thought, is based on ourthoughts and is made of our thoughts"* (Buddha 563 - 486 B.C.). Founder ofBuddhism.

79

thoughts". And, William Shakespeare[32] wisely claimed that "There is no such thing as good or bad; it is human thought that makes it appear so".

We are continuously interpreting reality, based on our past experiences, present motivations and future expectations. We create filters or schemes with which we value and give meanings to the events that surround us and concern us. AsEpictetus said [33]*"It is not the things that happen that disturbus, but the opinion we have of them"*. Thoughts determine our emotions; emotions form the basis of our actions and actions determine our behavior. If the behavior is repeated, it will become a habit, and this habit will become an automatism. If, for example, I suffer from a fear of olives and whenI have to face a social situation, such as a company cocktail party, where there is bound to be an appetizer with olives, and my thoughts turn to my weaknesses, to being blocked, to thinking that everyone will notice my ridiculous fear, to believing that I will lose all credibility..., I will be overcome with an emotion of fear. I will be overcome by an emotion of fear, of inferiority and possibly my prophecy will be fulfilled...I will be blocked, or I will be visibly and strangely agitated, Iwill blush, my throat will dry up and I will feel intense anxiety.And, worst of all, my fear, as it feeds back, will be even moreintense the next time. My fear will have grown fatter.

If after a failure in a task, you think: *"I am a useless person who does not do anything well; it is not worth even trying"*; your emotions and behavior will be very different than if you think: *"Well, I did not get the results I expected, but that does not make me useless, it only shows that I am a humanbeing who makes mistakes, like everyone else; I will see whatI can learn from this experience to take it into account next time"*. In the first case, it is not surprising that feelings of depression appear and the behavior is one of abandonment,while in the second case one may feel worried and discouraged, but these feelings will not be intense and incapacitatingenough to prevent solving the problem, moving on and learning how to do better for the next time.

4.11.2 The six principles of the Rational Emotive Model

---

[32] William Shakespeare (1564 - 1616). British writer.
[33] Epictetus of Phrygia (55 - 135). Greek philosopher. Stoic school

1) **Thought is the main determinant of human emotions:** Events or other people, although they may con-trib-ute, do not make us feel bad or good, but we do it ourselves depending on how we interpret the events and things that pass through our minds.

2) **Dysfunctional thinking is the main cause of emotional discomfort:** For example: if one morning on your way to work, you find that your car has a flat tire, it is up to you to feel angry (thinking how unfair life is to you, how unlucky you are...), or anxious (thinking that you will be late, that your boss will be angry, thathe will think of firing you...), or simply upset (thinking *"what can I do, I will have to change the tire and deal with the consequences as best I can"*). In the same way, if, in the presence of any emotional problem, fears, anxiety, relationship problems, etc., we analyze what is going through that person's mind at any given moment, we will see how what they are saying to themselves is causing them to feel one way or another. Being the thoughts what is feeding and maintaining their discomfort.

3) **We feel according to what we think:** To end an emotional problem, we have to start by doing ananalysis of our thoughts. If the discomfort is a productof irrational thinking, the best thing we can do is to change that thinking. In fact, it is the only thing we canchange, since we cannot directly change emotions or stop feeling bad just because we want to.

4) **Multiple factors, both genetic and environmentalinfluences (education, religion, etc.), are at the origin of irrational thinking: In** fact, human beings seem to have a natural tendency towards irrational (illogical and non-constructive) thinking, where the culture in which we live shapes the specific content of those beliefs.

5) Despite **the existence of past influences, the rational emotive model emphasizes present influences:** Since these are responsible for the fact that the distress has continued over time, despite the fact that past influences have ceased to exist. The main cause ofemotional discomfort has nothing to do with the way inwhich these beliefs or ways of interpreting reality wereacquired, but with the fact of continuing to maintain them in the present. Thus, if a person evaluates his orher way of thinking and changes it in the present, his or her functioning and feelings will be very

different. That is to say, it is not essential -although it may help-to go to the origin; neither is it necessary to discover what happened in the past, since we can work directlyin the present moment.

6) **Although beliefs can be changed, that change is not necessarily going to happen easily:** Irrational beliefs are changed through an active and persistent effort to recognize, discuss and modify them, which is the rational emotive task and intervention.

Example:

Let's suppose that you are driving your vehicle calmly and a car overtakes you and honks its horn, in principle you do not know why it has done so, but you come to the subjective conclusion that the sound of the horn was directed at you. You can even interpret that it was because you made a maneuver that you should not have made. In reality, we are making inferences that may very well be wrong or incorrect.Perhaps the reality is as simple as, the person who has hon-ked has used the acoustic warnings with the intention of greeting an acquaintance, but our particular perception, our inference, has caused us a feeling of emotional discomfort.

However, true irrational beliefs consist in the evaluation we make of those inferences. For example, if you think, *"He honked his horn because I am a bad driver,"* it will produce a different feeling than if you think, *"He honked his horn to warn me of his intention to overtake and thereby contribute to traffic safety."* The main work of rational emotive intervention is to get to those thoughts and evaluative inferences, which are at the heart of irrational beliefs and subsequent emotional distress.

4.11.3 Appropriate and inappropriate negative emotions

Negative and inadequate feelings are defined as those that make adverse conditions and frustrations worse and prevent solving the problem or the cause of the discomfort. These include anxiety, depression, anger, guilt, shame, shame and emotional pain. As we have seen, these feelings are caused by irrational, illogical, negative thoughts or beliefs...

Adequate negative emotions are those that tend to occur when human desires and preferences are blocked and frustrated. In these cases, feelings can help people to minimize oreliminate the problem. That is, they set us in motion to solveit. Among them are fear, worry, sadness, anger, remorse, modesty and disappointment.

The rational emotive model helps people to replace their inappropriate negative emotions with appropriate negative emotions, so that, when faced with a conflictive situation, instead of feeling paralyzing anxiety, for example, you can feel only a concern that leads you to solve the problem.

4.11.4 Appropriate and inappropriate positive emotions

Positive emotions and feelings can also be inappropriate. For example, the feeling of grandiosity or superiority is a positive emotion because it makes a person feel good. However, it is based on an unrealistic perception of oneself and will ultimately lead to rejection and problems in relationships with others.

Appropriate positive feelings and emotions are the result of the satisfaction of human desires, goals and ideals. They include love, joy, pleasure, curiosity, happiness.

Secondary symptoms: People, when they feel and act, have at the same time certain thoughts about their feelings and behaviors and these thoughts lead them to have other fee- lings and other behaviors. Thus, for example, a person who feels sad about the loss of something valuable realizes that and values that feeling in some way.

When people feel emotionally unwell, they sometimes perceive their symptoms in a **tremendously absolutist way**, thinking things like, *"It's **terrible** that I'm depressed; I'm **weak and useless** for feeling this way, I **can't stand it**."* Thus, they develop a secondary symptom, such as depression from being depressed or feeling anxious. Thus, a person suffering, for example, from claustrophobia may feel anxious just thinking about an elevator, or thinking that they need togo into a cramped bathroom with no window. This stems frombelieving that feeling anxious is something **terrible** that should not happen to you. Therefore, if you have to get on atrain, you might wonder if you will also feel anxiety in that situation. This fear of everything being terrible (**"terribilitis"**) will cause a significant increase in his anxiety, so that the person will arrive at the train feeling anxious and end upalso having a phobia of trains without even realizing the process that has led him to that situation. Consequently, he or she may end up adding anxiety to a larger number of situations, contexts and scenarios. Thus, these secondary symptoms may become more severe and disabling than the primary symptoms.

4.11.5 Talking to oneself

Our internal language, what we say to ourselves, is more important than it may seem at first glance. In the section of this book "Tell me what you think and I will tell you what you feel" (page 57 of this chapter) we have shown how our thoughts (inner language) directly influence our feelings or emotions. In this case we are going to talk briefly about "self-instructions". I am referring to those catch phrases that can either elevate our self-esteem or leave it in a bad light. Imagine thefollowing scene:

> Miriam has had a splendid day, she has finished adjusting the "Debits and Credits" of the income statement of all the Departments she is in charge of; they have called her from the dry cleaners to tell her that her dress, which she thought was irrecoverable, has been impeccable, as the red wine stain has not left a trace; her children are fine... "Everything is in order". She is, she does not know why, happy, radiant, with the strength to do anything... She thinks "Today I am going to try to drive at night, as Ferrán has a party, I will call him to tell him that today I will go to dinner with my friend Alicia, so he won't worry if I am late". He has not finished materializinghis decision and realizes that his mind is in continuous boiling. Ideas and feelings intertwine, collide,change direction, to suddenly turn around again... It's crazy, but she is determined *"I'm going to havedinner with my dear friend Alicia and I'm going to drive home at night!*
>
> *Suddenly*, you become aware that all that chaos of positive thinking begins to crumble. His good intentions fall as if they were dominoes lined up to that end. And in his mind, he begins to hear one of the mantras he fears most (self-instruction) *"You can't..., you can't"*. The phrase is now a fixed frame

that occupies all his thoughts. Soon more still fra-
mes come to life and follow in rapid succession,
changing the phrases for others of the same type.
Suddenly she puts down the phone on her desk,
which she had picked up to call Ferrán, and her
thoughts now circle around these three phrases:
*"How could you think that you could?" "You're a fai-
lure" "If you drive tonight, the same thing will happen to you that has happened the last few times...
You'll have to call someone to come and rescue you".*

In this case, you will agree with me, that the prognosis, if this
internal language is maintained, predicts a bad ending. For it is
clear that **"every sentence that passes through your mind
is a reinforcement for your success or failure to become
a reality".**

Miriam, using the **Thought Debate** technique (developed in
previous pages), will be able to change that language, those
phrases or self-instructions, for a more positive register such
as: *"I know that I might have a hard time on the way back,
but today I can", "If other people have been able to overcome
their fears, I can too", "If, in the end, I have to call Ferrán
halfway, I will call him, but I am going to try", "I can do it".*
The thought debate should be accompanied by an upright pos-
ture, head held high and a firm and determined step, even if it
is feigned.

This pretending may seem absurd, but, believe it or not, it is a
fairly widespread technique in clinical psychology, for example, in some cases such as in the beginning of a depression,
the patient is asked that, starting tomorrow when he/she gets
up, he/she must pretend to be a person without depression
(technique of acting as if). This means that: he/she has to go
out to do the shopping, even if at the beginning it is only to
get the bread (which implies: having to clean him/herself,
comb his/her hair, wear street clothes...); interact with people, even if it is only the essential, such as talking to the baker
to ask for a loaf of bread; return a greeting... All this pretending forces the person to break with the routines that start to
chain him/her to his/her depression. This is the technique of
acting as if. In this case, acting as if he/she did not have depression.

The danger of depressive behaviors (staying in bed, not worrying about hygiene or image, losing interest in interaction
with others, or in what is happening in the outside world...) is

that the longer the person suffers from depression, the more he/she clings to his/her depressive way of fee-ling, being and being. Therefore, it becomes a priority to break, as soon as possible, the routines, the programs of behavior, that weigh down and sink the person, in a progressive way, towards an endless pit.

This being so, and returning to Miriam, it is a priority to begin to change the routines, thoughts and behaviors that chain her to her phobia. I am not proposing a radical and fulminant change, as I have never agreed with shock or extreme[34] im-plosive therapies, but we must do what we can to change the behavioral patterns (behavioral programs) that apparently have become deeply rooted in Miriam's mind (more on beha-vioral programs later).

4.12 Neuro Linguistic Programming (PNL)

PNL is a model, not a theory, its purpose is to model what works, it is a system that teaches us how we structure infor-mation to build our reality and how to apply that knowledge in our relationship with our environment.

When we perceive information, in order to store it, we have to encode it by creating maps in our brain (as programs) thatsim-ulate a representation of what we have perceived. When we receive new information, it is compared with what we have stored, producing an integration based on our beliefs, expe-riences, knowledge and expectations, this will cause the map to be continuously rebuilt. Through verbal and non-verbal lan-guage, we can express our reality, and know how others con-struct theirs. If we know how someone constructs their reality we can redirect and influence their reconstruction. PNLhelps us to interpret, understand and improve human behavior.

- **Programming:** These are schemes of mental functio-ning determined by: the way we perceive, filter, feel emotionally and organize the information that reaches us both externally and internally (behavioral patterns).

- **Neuro:** Our behavior is related to external events, but passing through neurological processes such as: vision, hearing, smell, taste and touch.

---

[34] Implosive therapy, or flood therapy, is a technique used in psychology and psychiatry, where the patient is subjected to a direct exposure with no possibility of escape or avoid-ance, e.g., a person who is afraid of needles isput in a room full of shelves with syringes.

- **Linguistics:** Language is the structure that serves to organize our thoughts and is one of the vehicles of communication (both verbal and non-verbal).

PNL emerged from the work of Richard Bandler and John Grinder. These authors combined their knowledge of mathematics, computer science, psychology and linguistics. They observed that there are people who have a natural talent forcommunication and human relationships influencing the behavior of others. They decided to analyze the success of Milton Erickson, Virginia Satir and Fritz Perls, along with otherprestigious psychologists and therapists, who achieved extra- ordinary changes in people's behavior. When Bandler and Grinder asked the reference professionals what they did to achieve these results, they found that they themselves did not know what it was that made people give them so much credibility and trust them so much. Richard and John decidedto study conscientiously the way these therapists work and todo so, they recorded the verbal and non-verbal communication they used with their patients. They realized that they adapted to the particularities and differential idiosyncrasies ofeach of their patients, so that no two interventions were everthe same. The study of communication modeling, developedby Grinder and Bandler, was the beginning of the PNL process. In this approach, the concern ceases to be on the "**con-tents**" and the interest is directed to the concrete **form**, in the **here and now**, and in **HOW** people **construct their experience.**

We are not going to explore in depth the PNL model, since that would correspond to another moment, but we are goingto expose those concepts and fundamentals that will help usto explain and understand how the mind works in the formation of a phobia, in its maintenance and in its extinction or elimination.

4.13 How is the experience constructed?

a. **The environment: It** can be constituted by the origins of external or internal stimulation, it is the first link. Our inner environment has a lot to do with our level of neurotransmitters, enzymes and hormones, which are responsible for a large part of our mood and attitude. The external environment refers to all the stimuli that come from outside our body.

b. **Perceptions:** These are the physical stimulations that are picked up by our sensory receptors, being encoded in our brain. We have receptors for sight, hearing, touch, taste and smell. These signals are assembled into units called "internal moments", these are meaningless, as they are simple representations of the original signals.

c. **The present state:** To give them meaning, the brain needs to compare the new moments with previously processed ones (memory). The integration of the new moment in memory will give rise to a new meaning, a new subjective reality that corresponds to our present state.

d. **The desired state:** It is composed of: our beliefs Whatis important to me; our values Why are these beliefs important to me; and our expectations How or when will I achieve these expectations or values?

e. **Emotions:** They are the result of the comparison of the present state with the desired state, the comparison of the meaning we are giving at this moment with the beliefs, values and expectations we have. When our present state and the desired state are close, then, the emotions are satisfactory, when they are far away the emotions are of suffering, there are no good or bad emotions, there are emotions that are close or far awayfrom what we expect.

f. **Reality:** Our brain, to create reality, combines the present state, the desired state and emotions. It is a subjective reality that has been formed through the selection of perceived stimulation and the filters of our memory, our beliefs, values and expectations. The way in which we manifest that reality is through our behavior, the choice of behavior, of the response we will give will be determined by our subjective reality.

When we begin a process of internalization and change to seek alternative solutions to our problems, we must keep in mind the precepts that organize mental processes. Here are some of these precepts:

a. **Every thought or idea produces a physical reaction**. All thoughts affect all functions of the organism, examples:

   • Worrying thoughts trigger changes in the gastric

juice of the stomach, which in the long term can
lead to ulcers.
- Angry thoughts increase the level of adrenaline in
the blood, producing various changes in the body.
- Anxious and fearful thoughts increase the heart
rate.

b. **All ideas that have a strong emotional content almost always reach the unconscious** (the feeling
mind). Once accepted these ideas continue to produce
the same bodily reaction over and over again. It is necessary, therefore, to break this vicious circle somewhere if we do not want to fall again and again intothe
same psychophysiological or psychosomatic responses
(anxiety symptoms).

c. Once **an idea has been accepted by the unconscious mind, it remains until another idea replaces
it.** This rule is associated with the following: The longer
an idea remains, the greater is the resistance to its being
replaced by another new idea. Once an idea hasbeen accepted, it tends to remain, and the longer it actsand re-
peats itself, the more it tends to become a habitual way
of thinking. This is how habits are formed, good or bad.

d. **We have patterns of thought and action**. Note well:
"Every action is preceded by a thought". If we want to
modify our actions, we have to start by modifying our
thoughts. We accept certain facts as true. We accept that
the sun rises in the east and sets in the west, evenwhen
it is cloudy and we cannot see it. We have manythought
patterns that are incorrect and yet they have become
fixed (engraved) in our mind. There are peoplewho at
critical moments ingest large amounts of alcohol, smoke,
or consume toxic substances to performefficiently. These
behaviors are not appropriate, be- cause instead of helping, they harm, but the idea is there, and it is a fixed
pattern of thought. We will surelyencounter internal op-
position if we want to replace them with new ideas.

e. **An emotionally induced symptom, if it persists
long enough, tends to cause organic changes.** Medical science recognizes that more than 60% of human
illnesses are psychosomatic. It may happen that the
function of an organ or part of the body has been dis-
turbed by the reaction of the nervous system to negative ideas held by the unconscious. We do not mean by

this that every person who complains of an illness is emotionally ill or neurotic. There are illnesses caused by germs, parasites, viruses, etc. We are an inseparable whole of mind and body! If you continually fear that your health will weaken, if you constantly talk about your stomach nerves or your migraines due to tension, in the long run organic changes may occur that sustain those ailments.

f. **Each suggestion put into practice decreases resistance to successive suggestions.** The longer a mental tendency lasts, the easier it is to continue. Oncea habit is formed it tends to acquire permanence and therefore greater resistance to change. When the unconscious has accepted a suggestion, it becomes easier to accept new suggestions and put them into practice. Advertising, marketing and partly clinical hypnosis are based on this principle.

4.13.1 Behavioral programs

One of the skills or competencies that characterizes human beings from other living beings is their ability to learn and adapt to change.

We could say that a behavioral program is the set of routines that, repeated in the same sequence and order, offer us an invariable result. This set of routines becomes a behavioral program once its execution is achieved automatically and unconsciously.

This resource or behavioral program allows human beings to execute an automated task (driving a vehicle) at the same time that, for example, we can hold a conversation (multitasking) without too many difficulties. For this to be a reality, itis essential that the steps of the task being performed have reached a high level of automation, otherwise we are likely to make mistakes in the execution of the task or lose the threadof the conversation.

Examples:

g. People who have been working in a factory for years, always using the same machine, and performing the same sequences of movements (routines) over and over again, can repeat these automatic tasks while theirmind is skiing in the Swiss Alps.

h. If for a long time we have always put, let's say, the toothpaste tube in the same place and someone chan-ges its place, if we are doing another task simultane-ously, we can spend some time feeling around unsuc-cessfully in the area where the toothpaste had usually been and we were expecting to find it.

The point is that since we are born, we shape and store beha-vioral programs for absolutely everything, some simpler (like finding the toothpaste) and others more complex. To prove it to you I am going to share with you some of the thousands of behavioral programs in my repertoire. In this case: the pro-gram that allows me to prepare my breakfast every morning.

I have been living in the same house for more than twenty years, so I could walk through the rooms and rooms of the house without too much trouble (I think), with my eyes clo-sed. Every morning, to prepare my breakfast, I have to go downstairs to the kitchen and the living room.

The point is, I don't go downstairs consciously thinking that when the stairs are finished, I have to open the door, located to my right, that gives me access to the kitchen. Nor do I have to make an effort to establish the sequences to find therefrig-erator, open it, take the milk container, fill a glass, putit in the microwave, pour cereal in a bowl... All these steps are exe-cuted by themselves, without thinking, they have been auto-mated in a program. It is true that my mind struggled at the beginning to learn sequentially each and every one of the movements that aim to prepare breakfast, but overtime my mind has been generating routines, in order to freemy con-sciousness (saving effort) so that I can think about other things while executing a task that has become a pro- gram. So, as I walk down the stairs and open the door... Mymind is thinking "Today I have to go to the University... WhenI get out of class I have to remember to go through AcademicManage-ment to...".

You may be asking yourself, "What about me, how do you pre-pare your breakfast? Well, the truth is that you are absolutely right, but it was just an example to show you that ourbrain is a real machine for making programs, because its maxim is to be governed by the "law of parsimony[35]" or the lawof minimum

---

[35] The law of parsimony, or the law of least effort, is sometimes misinterpreted, as some people think that it is the law of lazy and lazy people, but itis not, because what this law

effort. The truth is that up to this point it seemsa great advantage that we have programs for everything andfrom then on, we forget. This reality would be great if all thosemechanized programs, canned and stored in our memory, would adjust perfectly and forever to any situation, place or event, but today's habits change for tomorrow, what is nor- mal and accepted in this culture is not in another and, for what yesterday we were applauded today we are criticized ...In short, we are forced to modify our behavioral programs continuously. The truth is that we generally do so without toomany problems. Things get more complicated when it comesto the two initial elements that make up our behavioral pro- grams:

rational mind + objective to be achieved

Example: I go running every morning (rational mind) because running is healthy (goal to achieve = health).

The emotional variable is added. This new behavioral program formula would be composed of:

rational mind + objective to be achieved + emotional mind

Example: I go running every morning (rational mind) because running is healthy (goal to achieve = health).
and if I don't do it I feel that I am useless and a failure (emotional mind).

Maybe it can be a help, to better explain what I want to express, if our friend Manel gives us a hand:

Manel has been integrating in his mind behavioral programs associated with the phobia he suffersfrom. Let's see some of them:

- If he sees or thinks about a tunnel, he feels fear and anxiety, so he tries to avoid thinking about anything that has to do with going into a tunnel with the car.
- If you think about taking a route through a tunnel, you immediately feel fear and anxiety, so you avoid the possibility by studying alternative routes. When this happens, an unbearable fee-

---

aims to achieve the same results with the leastpossible effort. It could be compared to efficiency.

ling of guilt invades him and he feels like a wreck.

We could continue giving more examples of programs elaborated by Manel, but I think that the idea has already been understood. As long as Manel has as response mechanisms these behavioral programs, he will continue to repeat the avoidance and/or escape from the routes where there are tunnels, in order not to suffer anxiety crises. Manel is afraid of his fear.

So, what should I do?

I guess you have already guessed it... Manel has to change his programs for others that are more adaptive.

And how is that done? Well, let's continue until we see how.

. *"Life is not the life one lived,*
but the one that remembers and
as he remembers it. "
Gabriel García Márquez[36]

Chapter 5

5 The visualization technique in imagination

The visualization technique in imagination is a process that allows us to relive past experiences, visually and emotionally, in order to make changes in those memories that cause us dissatisfaction or discomfort.

At the same time, the use of imagination facilitates the visualization of future situations, which are yet to come, thus allowing us to rehearse the experience without it ever taking place. Although it may seem unusual, according to Buddha[37], we are a product of what we think, and it is clear that images occupy a large space in our thoughts and in our memory.

5.1 Visualization as a resource for overcoming phobias

Visualization is a resource that facilitates the reconstruction of a reality adjusted to our desires and expectations. As we progress in learning visualization, the situations we want to work on can be brought to life, in order to experience them with a greater degree of reality.

If our experience is built from the information we receive through our senses and its subsequent integration with our previous knowledge, then we can also reconstruct our reality by modifying the information that interests us through visualization. The more real the event we are visualizing, the more we increase the probability of achieving the desired changes. An example of what I am trying to communicate to you is the

---

[36] Gabriel Garcia Marquez. He was born in Colombia (1927 - 2014). He was a Colombian writer and journalist. He received the Nobel Prize for Literature in 1982.

[37] *"Everything we are is the result of what we have thought, is based on our thoughts and is made of our thoughts"* (Buddha 563 - 486 B.C.). Founder of Buddhism.

following:

> If a person had a traumatic childhood experience with a dog in which the dog growled and bared its teeth at him and has never since approached a similar animal. He has built up the belief that these animals are dangerous and not to be trusted. This circumstance reinforces the fact that he does not approach them and, therefore, he cannot corroborate or refute that idea, which will not only maintainhis fear, but will feed on his own fear, increasing over time. With visualization we can get that personto see himself playing in a fun way with a dog (we can start with a puppy) sharing tenderness and companionship. If he feels the visualization intensely, he will be changing his mental program aboutthese animals and at the same time he will be re- constructing his memories and therefore a part of his reality.

With visualization we can change our emotions (feelings) and face the situation in a neutral way, stop feeling it as a challenge, and later live it, if desired, as an achievement or a triumph.

All our thoughts produce results. If we have creative and positive thoughts, we will have creative and positive results. If, on the other hand, our thoughts are negative, we will have negative results. It is clear that we have to change the way we think and see the world if we want to achieve more adaptive results[38]. Suggestion or autosuggestion combined with our imagination can change our reality by changing the way we perceive, see and feel.

Our memories can be the basis of our emotional feeling, because the experiences remembered (relived) can influence our way of perceiving and therefore of living. People who onlycling to their negative memories have a very difficult time finding happiness, because their entire vision of the reality around them is tainted with negativity and defeat.

Perhaps, at this point, you are wondering *how to promote the memories that you want, the positive memories that help me to grow and live peacefully? And in this case, to get away from my phobia.*

---

[38] Albert Einstein summarized this idea in the following sentence: "If you are looking for different results, don't always do the same thing".

What if I told you that it is much easier than you might suspect. Did you know that most of our memories are not one hundred percent true? Well, I'm not saying that, if you remember being in your childhood, for example, in an old country house in the Empordà it's not true, I'm sure it was, but...

And if I ask you to try to remember what the room was like where you were sleeping that week. Imagine that you are in the bed where you slept, and I ask you to describe the ceiling of the bedroom. Suppose you don't remember what it was like, what do you think your mind will do in that situation? Above all, knowing that our mental functioning is governed by logic and coherence, is your mind going to leave the roomwithout a ceiling? In other words, is your mind going to acceptthat, while lying in bed, you will be looking at the sky, the moon and the stars? No, isn't it? What is going to promote your mental logic functioning, is to look for and put a ceiling that is related to the antiquity of the house, possibly white, with wooden beams

Curious to say the least... Curious, isn't it? Just in case you don't see it clearly, let me continue with the demonstration.

Imagine, while you are reading, that you enter that room of that old house and you turn on the light, instantly the room lights up, now direct your gaze to the switch with which you have turned on the light. I would like you to notice what that switch looks like, its shape, its color, its texture... That's it! You are doing very well... Now, without haste repeat this same visualization (now with your eyes closed) a couple of times more, I am sure you have found your particular versionof what that switch of that imaginary house looks like. You may ask... And how is that? Simply, because one of the waysour memory stores our memories is through images, so if we imagine through visualization that an event has occurred andwe reinforce it through repetition, in the end, our mind has trouble differentiating fact from fiction.

Many of the memories we have, from when we were little, area reconstruction that we make, by visualization, when we listen to a relative telling something, we did in our childhood. Aswe listen to the story, we visualize what that person describesand, at the same time, we build and integrate a memory in our memory, so, as I said a few lines above, we should not rely entirely on our memories, because many of them have been implemented, produced and completed from remnants of our own memories and versions of stories heard.

In my opinion, this anomaly in the elaboration, registration and recovery of our memories presents a great advantage, if what we want is to modify past memories that may be difficult or painful for us, or simply to train ourselves, through imagination, on how to face, for example, a job interview, thus reducing the possible tension. It is also true that, given this reality, one should question the value of the testimony offered by the witness of a criminal act. But that is another mat-ter....

You may think that how is it possible that I am talking about generic anomalies in our brain... Reality shows us that our wonderful thinking and feeling machine also has its deficiencies. Let's see if I can prove it....

5.2 The blindness of our emotions

Nowadays, as I have expressed in previous chapters, nobody doubts that in our mind we can identify two perfectly differentiated figurative rooms: in one is the reason where we find the intellect, logic, our conscious thinking, reasonableness, ideas, (our cognitive area). ; in the other we locate the emotions, where joy, sadness, anger, fear are present. Would you believe me if I told you that our emotional part does not know how to distinguish reality from fiction? Difficult to accept, isn't it? In my argument I am going to start from an everyday fact such as watching a movie...

Analyze for a moment what happens when we are watchinga movie. Our rational part knows that what we are seeing is not real. It knows that they are actors and actresses playinga role. We even know, for example, that the protagonist, an 8-year-old girl who dies in the film, is now 30 years old and ishappily married to a successful director In short, she is still alive today... So, if rationally we are clear about this information, how is it possible that, when we see her die during the screening, we end up crying with grief? How is it possible that,knowing that she is an actress playing a role and that in reality it is a fictitious death, we are flooded with sadness? The question is quite simple: our emotional part, "which is in its own things", does not distinguish the fictitious facts from thereal ones.

If the movie was a scary movie and following the same reasoning: if we look at the screen, as an example: a "zombie" chasing someone, we are overcome with panic (emotional area), when we know, if we use our rational part, that underthat terrible appearance of the living dead there are hours and hours of professional make-up.

In fact, we classify films according to their capacity to generate emotions in the viewer. We will say it is "good" when it makes us laugh (emotion of Joy), or cry (emotion of Sadness), or produces panic (emotion of Fear), or violence (emotion of Anger). Generally, the movies that we do not like, or that bore us are those that leave us indifferent "They have not touched any of our emotions".

5.3 Taking advantage of our emotional blindness

This mismatch between our intellectual reasoning and our emotions opens an immense window in the treatment of phobias... For it allows us to reprogram our mind, replacing the program that is dysfunctional, for example, the maladaptive response of avoidance, panic and flight of a person beforea plate of olives, with a new program where the memories incorporated, through visualization in imagination, allow himto react normally to the presence of olives. Visualization in imagination allows us to break the established association, asan anchor, between the phobic stimulus and the appearanceand maintenance of anxiety, and to create another anchor where the person responds to the phobic stimulus without fear or anxiety responses. In short, it allows us to change ananomalous program for a new totally adaptive one.

In any case, let's take advantage of those little misalignments of the mind, for our own benefit, and continue with "How to get the most out of our imagination".

5.4 How to make a visualization in imagination

The procedure of visualization in imagination is simple, we only need a comfortable and quiet place, where we know thatwe have some time in which no one will disturb us.

Sitting on a sofa, or lying on a bed, we loosen our muscles and let all the weight of our body rest on the sofa or bed where we are. With our eyes closed, after taking several deepbreaths, we start by visualizing a place that we have previously associated with relaxation, such as: a white sandy beach, crystal clear water and a palm tree or a clearing in the mountains, next to a stream, with trees and the smell offresh grass...

Once the place is chosen, if for example it is the beach, we enjoy watching the contrast between the blue of the sea and the blue of the sky, we follow the slow movement of the white clouds, which are like little pieces of cotton scattered in a disorderly way. We listen to the soft sound of the waves in their incessant coming and going. We may even be able to perceive that characteristic smell of the sea breeze. Enjoying all these sensations... When you feel that your mind and body are in a state of relaxation, go on to visualize now what you want to achieve: overcoming your irrational fears, changing the emotional perception of a memory, facing an exam or any other type of challenge you have set out to achieve.

The more you repeat the visualizations, the more you get used to them, the more you train and habituate your mind tothe situation you want to face or change. Without realizing it,you are doing, through visualization by imagination, a virtualtraining. Remember: our memory, if we have registered scenes we have heard through visualization, can store them as real experiences. I would like to end this paragraph with a phrase from Carlos Ruiz Zafón[39] *"Sometimes, the most real things only happen in the imagination"*.

The best thing about imagination is that besides beinga powerful and multipurpose tool, it is totally free, it isinfinite, and the limits are only set by you. Use it to growin a positive way, because it is one of the best resources, we human beings have, and it is always available.

5.5 Imagination: a multifunctional tool

I would not like to end this chapter without expanding on what I have said in previous points about imagination as a "powerful and multi-purpose tool". In addition to all the functions we have assigned so far to our visualization in imagination, I would also like you to see the benefit it can have, insuch disparate contexts and uses, as an instrument of evasion, since it provides you with the possibility of escaping from boring or extreme situations.

---

[39] Carlos Ruiz Zafón. He is a Catalan writer. Author of successful works such as "La sombra del viento", "El juego del Ángel" or "El laberinto de losespíritus", among others.

I am thinking about how people who have been deprived of their freedom (let's say kidnapped) have been able to endure their confinement in a cell without talking to anyone, without any news from the outside, without seeing natural light, for months or years... How have they managed not to end up in madness? I believe that those who have managed to survive such terrible situations are people who have clung to their imagination to escape the horror of that reality. While they were isolated, they used their imagination to be with their family, to enjoy nature, to enjoy watching a sunset, to talk, to feel and embrace their loved ones?

In fact, it is very clear to me that when someone states that "Only people who have a strong mind can overcome this type of situation" they are actually referring, perhaps unknowingly, to the fact that: "Only people who have known how to use visualization in imagination have been able to endure andovercome this type of terrible trauma".

Continuing with the many uses that can be attributed to visualization in imagination, have you ever wondered how it is possible that, from one day to the next, certain people show significant changes in their learning results on, for example, manual tasks? I think you are "imagining" the answer, aren't you...? Well, those people accelerate their learning process because they train in imagination: visualizing themselves in the execution of the task they want to perform.

5.6 Mirror neurons

In this regard I am going to talk to you about mirror neurons. This is the name given to a series of specific neurons located between the parietal and frontal lobes of the brain. These neurons are activated when we observe someone performingan activity. In 1996, the authors Gallese, Fadiga, Fogassi and Rizzolatti[40] studied, in a group of apes, the brain activation that occurred when the monkeys observed what another of their peers was doing. They concluded that: the same neurons were activated in the monkey performing an action as inthe monkeys observing it, hence the name mirror neurons.

This discovery opened a new area of knowledge in learning processes, as it shows that the simple fact of observing how a

---

[40] The bibliographic reference for this study is: Gallese, V., Fadiga, L., Fogassi, L. and Rizzolatti, G. (1996). Action recognition in the premotor cor-tex. *Brain* 119, 593-609.

task is performed mobilizes a series of specific neurons thatwill facilitate the acquisition of new learning and/or reinforcethose already acquired. If we visualize in imagination how toperform a task, we are activating neural circuits that facilitatethe learning of that activity. It is for this reason that there arepeople who, from one day to the next, present extraordinaryadvances in the learning of complex tasks. This provokes in those who witness these facts the typical phrase *"It's not likeyou've been practicing all night"*. Surely the result is not dueto physical practice, because in few cases someone spends allnight training, but possibly we will find people who spend timeand more time thinking over and over, visualizing in their imagination, what they are trying to learn, or what they in- tend to do.

5.7 Visualization and creativity

Although there are undoubtedly many more uses that we can attribute to visualization in the imagination, I want to finish (because I do not want to get heavy with this topic) relating this technique with creativity. To do so, I am going to introduce Vickie the Viking in these pages[41]. I beg your pardon for my boldness, but I think we have already had a few pages of confidence.

I know it may seem to you that we are regressing tochildhood, but the character may be a good example of the idea I am sharing with you. In case you don't remember, or you have never seen this series, Vickie solved complex situations or conflictive moments through imagination... When faced with a complicated situation, after a while of visualizing the problem, the solution would appear accompanied by littlestars and the word *"Eureka"*. This children's example, taken from a cartoon series, seems to me perfect to define how through visualization we can reach the resolution of problemsthat are difficult to solve, either because of: difficulty of access, lack of material or economic resources, or even becauseit is dangerous to rehearse in a real way without having clearand defined the steps to follow, for example: a gymnast whovisualizes, over and over again, the movements to be performed to achieve a triple somersault.

Another important feature about visualization in imaginationis

---

[41] Wickie the Viking is a cartoon series made in 1974 thanks to a co-production between Japan and Germany, where the adventures of a young Viking and his brilliant ideas are narrated.

that the only barriers you may encounter are yours alone.

So, the question is... Are you going to get the most out of the visualization technique in imagination, or are you going to continue to keep this wonderful skill, or resource, lost and forgotten in some corner of your head?

"Technique is the effort
to save effort".
José Ortega y Gasset[42]

Chapter 6

6   Anxiety management techniques

In the following, we will describe, based on what we have said so far, different techniques and guidelines for treating phobias. It is not necessary that we have to use all of them. The evolution of the problem will serve us as a guide to implement or modify the techniques we are using in order to adapt them to the idiosyncrasy of each person and to the specific situation we are facing. For example, in the case of any phobia, it is essential to work meticulously on cognitive restructuring (everything we have talked about Albert Ellis, ERT and thought debate...). The objective is to modify the ideas and erroneous beliefs on the magnification of the dan-ger that the person presupposes that it will happen to him (sometimes without having had previous experience that corroborates or justifies his fear, example: Manel does not go through any tunnel because he assumes that he is going to suffer an anxiety attack).

6.1 Anxiety in itself is not dangerous

One of the greatest difficulties in dealing with anxiety is the fear of suffering from it, of suffering from the symptoms that arise due to the fear of losing control, of having a heart attack, of people noticing that something "strange" is happening to us. To begin with, we should understand and accept that anxiety in itself is not dangerous, it is only a response activation mechanism. In fact, if we are not affected by a se rious coronary or respiratory pathology, anxiety alone will not cause us to suffer a heart attack or respiratory arrest. We must have clear goals to achieve, trust in our own resources that we already have and in those that we will seek, find andimplement. We must be able to verify how once we put thesestrategies into action and begin to pay no attention to anxiety, its

---

[42] José Ortega y Gasset (1883 - 1955). Born in Madrid. Philosopher and professor of psychology, ethics and logic.

symptoms will stop appearing and if they do, their duration will be shorter and of less intensity.

Another important issue: It is necessary that any challenge overcome, no matter how small or partial it may be, we see it as a victory and not as a failure. Let me give you an example:

Georgina panics about elevators

> Georgina has avoided elevators, or anything like them, for three years. Even being in a lobby where there are elevators already makes her heart race and her hands sweat. Ever since she suffered a panic attack (when the elevator stops- ped between two floors), which ended in a visit tothe ER, she has been avoiding any confined, enclosed space.
>
> Today, after getting up the courage, having psyched herself up and with the help of herpsychologist, she is going to face her fear... She is going to visit her friend Anna, who works in a photography studio on the 11th floor of a buildingon the Diagonal. When she arrives at the entrance, she is surprised by her apparent calmness, as she has been much more nervous sinceyesterday morning (which is when she decided totake the step), than now that she is crossing thethreshold of the office building. It is not that she is totally calm, but...
>
> She is in front of the door of one of the elevators that will allow her to go up to see her friend Anna. Although she notices that the palms of her hands are starting to get wet, she knows that she is going to make it... She puts her index finger on the call button... She feels delighted, because yesterday she would have bet that: that simple gesture would mean her life, she thought that such a simple action for any person, for her would be an unreachable achievement. "*I can, I can, I can, I can,*" she says to herself.
>
> His incipient joy and triumphalism vanish at the same moment that, when the doors that give him access to enter open, he sees three people who surely come from the Parking.

Georgina hesitates (she expected to be alone). She feels that she is being watched with the sameintensity as she feels her heart racing. Surprisingly, she doesn't know how it happened, but she has entered. A kind of cloud envelops her. She feels watched... She doesn't really know if she ismore anxious and worried about what the occupants of the elevator might think (who are surelyrealizing her fear), or because the cabin is so small, or because the elevator might fall... Whileshe thinks that it will be impossible to reach the 11th floor, she notices how the elevator slows down, stops and, accompanied by a sound similarto a "CLING", the doors open (SIXTH FLOOR).
Georgina doesn't think about it, she rushes out of the elevator, as if she wants to disappear, and decides to walk up the five floors that separate her from her meeting with her friend Anna.

There are many interpretations that can be made of this episode experienced by Georgina. The question is, how would you classify the experience? Do you think it has been a success? Or do you think it was a failure? (positive - negative)

Remember that our thoughts are the basis of our emotions and that fear is one of the primary emotions.

6.1.1 If Georgina perceives the experience as a defeat and her thoughts are: *"I am a failure... I already knew it...I don't even know why I dared... I will never succeed"...*She will surely go back on her way to face and over- come her fears (negative vision).

6.1.2 *On the other hand*, if you take it as a fruitful experience and the thoughts that go through your mind are: *"My God, who would have told me that I could reach the sixth floor, when yesterday I would not even have been able to press the call button... I am happy and con- tent... I know I am going to make it... Next day I will go up two more floors, or I will reach the end..." (positive vision).* (positive view).

It looks like there is going to be a big difference in the forecast between option a) and option b), don't you think?

On the other hand, he should find in us, psychology professionals and especially in his family and friends, all the under-standing and support that is possible. Our communicationmust be empathic and our language positive. The relationshipmust be relaxed, we must refuse and avoid situations of forced help. We must always know when to stop without lookingfor limit sit-uations, it is better to go little by little and advancestep by step and with a firm foot. To empathize means to understand the fears of the person who receives our help andat the same time to show him/her a wide range of resources,strategies, tech-niques and possibilities that give him/her confidence and moti-vation to succeed in his/her fight against his/her phobia.

6.2 Initial symptom management

Initially we will focus on overcoming the physiological sym-ptoms, as they are the most annoying and disabling, once they disappear the person suffering from the phobia will be more capable and competent to face future challenges that, progres-sively, we will agree and overcome.

The autonomic nervous system is responsible for regula-ting the respiratory, cardiovascular and endocrine systems, assisting the digestive process and regulating body tempera-ture. This system comprises in turn:

- The **sympathetic nervous** system, responsible for activa-tion and alertness responses and therefore for anxiety.

- The **parasympathetic nervous system**, responsible for slowing down and balancing the alterations produced by the activation of the sympathetic system.

The sooner we activate the parasympathetic system, the soo-ner we will eliminate anxiety. It is necessary to learn to iden-tify the first symptoms of anxiety in order to implement, as soon as possible, strategies to stop them. It is necessary to think that, if the parasympathetic nervous system is mobili-zed, before the sympathetic system is active and at full ca-pacity, there will be more possibilities to dampen it. The signs are presented by association, or anchoring, when exposed to situations or places that have produced anxiety through pre-vious experiences (example with Manel: going to have a drink on the terrace of a bar). Internal changes in bodily and mental functions occur: onset of increased heart rate, increased breathing, sweating, body tension, recurrent thoughts ofworry or fear. It is important that the person learns to recognize the symptoms of anxiety, but we must remember that, although the symptoms alone are not dangerous: **If self-observation turns into worry and obsession, we will be worsening the anxiety**.

6.3 Learning to breathe

Before going into this point, we should remember what we have explained here about our nerve center, specifically the medulla oblongata, which is in charge of automatically esta-blishing our breathing. So, if we ever interfere it should be to increase calmness and not to achieve the opposite. Breathing correctly is essential to manage anxiety. We must learn to re-store the optimal level of oxygen in the blood, that is, we must learn **when to** control our breathing and **how to** do it:type of breathing, frequency, rhythm, pauses.

In the beginning, the most important thing is the when and the how. This implies learning different tasks of varying diffi-culty, which we will gradually acquire and incorporate through daily practice.

- **When:** At the first signs of anxiety. As soon as the acti-vation of the sympathetic nervous system and its bodily manifestations are perceived: onset of increased heart rate, increased respiration, sweating, body tension, etc.

- **How**: Through controlled breathing. At the beginning of exposure to anxiogenic situations or places, or when slightly noticing the first physiological symptoms of an- xi-ety (seconds and minutes are always approximate):

   - Take a mental count of 4 (4 seconds).
   - Hold the air for a count of 4 (4 seconds).
   - Release the air for a count of 6 (6 seconds).
   - Repeat 12 times (for 3 minutes).

- The ideal is to inhale air through the nose and exhale through the mouth, but if you have a cold or for some other cause we cannot do it this way, do not worry, it willstill be effective. It is important to consider that, while weare pay-ing attention to how to do a proper breathing, westop fo-cusing on the symptoms of anxiety.

   When the symptoms are stronger, for example: in an an-guish crisis:
   - If possible, stop what you are doing and sit down.

- Hold your breath for 10 seconds without having previously taken any deep breaths.
- When you reach 10, let the air out by mentally saying to yourself the word "calm" or "relax" or "tranquility".
- Take a mental count of 4 (4 seconds).
- Hold the air for a count of 4 (4 seconds).
- Release the air for a count of 6 (6 seconds).
- Repeat 8 times (4 to 6). If it persists, start from 1 to 7.

The greatest benefit will be obtained if the breathing is done abdominally, but as we have mentioned above, for the moment we cannot wait for the person to learn this type of breathing to do these exercises. As it becomes easier to perform abdominal breathing, normal breathing can be substituted for abdominal breathing (this helps to prevent and/or control hyperventilation).

Next, we will show the abdominal breathing. It is called so, not because it is breathed with the abdomen, in fact it is donewith the lower part of the lungs -with the diaphragm- but theimpression is that it is executed with the abdomen when thisarea is mobilized.

6.4 Abdominal breathing

To practice, choose a time when there are no interruptions. Select, if possible, a dimly lit place with no distracting sounds. To start practicing:
- Adopt a seated position. If you are unable to breathe properly, you can start in a reclining or lying position.
- Loosen clothing, belts, or other garments that may be tight, especially around the waist or abdomen.
- Adopt a comfortable position and place one hand on the chest and the other on the abdomen with the little finger just above the navel.
- Breathe in through the nose. Breathe out through the nose or mouth. If you have a problem that prevents you from inhaling through your nose, do it through your mouth, but do not open it too wide.
- Breathe in through your nose for 3 or 4 seconds using your diaphragm. The abdomen will rise, you will feel it with the hand you have rested on it. Do not raise your shoulders or practically move your thorax.
- Exhale slowly through the nose or mouth for 3 to 4 seconds. The abdomen will return to its original position.

Pause briefly before breathing in again, thus breathing about 8 times per minute. If you breathe even more slowly, no problem, but if this rhythm is too slow for the person in question, you can start with a faster oneof 12 breaths per minute in which inspiration and expiration last 2 seconds each. After that, you will have to gradually approach the rhythm of 8 or less breaths perminute.

Practice controlled breathing twice a day, at a rate of 10 minutes each time. During the first four days, practice with your eyes closed and the remaining days with your eyes open.

6.5 Distraction and fun

It may be the case that the phobia originates anxiety states long before facing the situation that causes the phobia (phobic stimulus). Remember Monica: long before it was timeto go to her parents' farmhouse, she began to feel ill, the mere thought that in a few hours or a couple of days she would be exposed to a situation where the risk of encountering a grasshopper is high, triggered all the responses of her sympathetic nervous system.

What maintains anxiety and fear is the fixation of our mind with the perception of threat and danger in relation to the symptoms and their consequences. We have to direct our thinking towards distracting tasks, to get out of the circular loop of anxiety, performing tasks that require our attention to avoid entering it. The following tasks and distractions are aimed at breaking that spiral, or circle of thought, which generates anxiety long before we face the phobic situation.

- **Distracting tasks:** Although, as we have seen in previous pages, humans are capable of performing several tasks at the same time (multitasking), it is evident that an overexertion and a distribution of concentration in the differentoccupations is needed. In order that the greatest weight ofattention does not continue to be focused on anxiety, we must look for distractions that are difficult or of great interest to us. Here are a few of them that can help us to shift our attention away from the perception of danger. Some may work better than others, depending on the personal characteristics of each subject and the situation or place where the action takes place:
    - Mentally count from 100 a1 in descending order from three to three: 100 - 97 - 94 - 91 - 88 - ...

- Add up the license plate numbers of cars passing on the street.
- Mentally review the ingredients and steps to prepare a cooking dish.
- Look up dictionary definitions of words whose meaning is unclear.
- Look for differences between two known people, both physically and personality-wise.
- Think about what the ideal vacation spot would be like.
- Humming the favorite song. It is better that it is in our language and that it is given rhythm and intonation, thus working with both cerebral hemispheres.
- Read something we like.
- Playing with the console or cell phone.
- Carry a purse with plenty of coins and count them.
- Carry a pocket calendar and start counting the days until the next party, the next tunnel, Christmas, etc., etc., etc.

- **Amusements:** We should initiate some activity or hobby that hinders the onset of anxiety. Just as we have learned to give anxiety responses, we must reverse this learning and redirect it to another task that occupies our time and thoughts. Excuses are often made saying that we do not feel like doing anything, that we do not have time, that we are tired. But to achieve a big change we have to start by making small changes and sometimes, to get control over our will, we have to start doing things we do not like. We know that time is relative and that having or not having it is a matter of priorities and, in this case, health should be ahead of other motivations.

  If we tell ourselves that we are tired, anxiety probably has a lot to do with it, what we refuse to do will keep us from achieving a satisfactory solution. It is true that it is diffi-cult for us to change our habits: The known gives us se-curity and the unknown makes us afraid, but anxiety has become a habit and paradoxically we need to do new things to banish it, even if at first it means feeling somewhat in-secure. Here are some examples of activities that can help:
  - Exercising or playing sports, preferably in company.
  - Organize your time, do not stay at home with nothing to do.
  - Plan weekends in advance.
  - Perhaps there is something we would like to learn.
  - Looking for a hobby that pleases us, we expose only some of the many that may be available:
    - Photography
    - Fishing

- Collect
- Model making
- Garden or orchard
- Cooking
- Painting or ceramics

6.6 Self-instructions

Children often talk to themselves out loud. They use language to guide their behavior, reinforce it and motivate themselves in its execution. With time, and unconscious repressions sponsored by the feeling of shame and *"what people will say"*, we stop doing it, but not because it is no longer effective. We are all accustomed to following orders and the word is one of the most powerful tools to convince us of something. Self- instructions influence how we feel and how we behave; if they are positive, they will generate feelings of well-being and adaptive behaviors. Who can we trust more than ourselves?

Anxiety originates in the mind and it is in the mind where we must work to manage it, we must convince ourselves that what happens to us is not dangerous, that other times we have had anxiety and we have overcome it, that every time it appears we know how to manage it better and that we will manage to win the battle. The ideal is that the self- instructions we give them aloud, but it can be embarrassing especially if there are people around us who can hear us. So, when we are not alone, we will use the internalized word, that is to say, say it to yourself mentally, but with a convincing and confident tone, you not only have to say it, but believe it. Next, we will show several examples of self-instructions, although the best thing is that each person constructs them for himself with his own language:

- Anxiety is not dangerous.
- It's annoying, but it will pass.
- It's not the first time it's happened to me and I've always gotten over it.
- I am going to focus on my breathing.
- I give too much importance to things.
- That thing that scares me so much, in the end, never happens.
- I always anticipate the worst without any proof.

6.7 Relaxation

Relaxation is the opposite side of anxiety, everyone likes to relax, but few people know how to do it at will. We have all heard on occasion, for example, when we are sitting in the dentist's chair and the dentist tells us *"Relax, you are very tense"* and we think *"Yes, and how do you do that by having your mouth open, listening to the hum of the drill and seeing how it approaches"*.

Relaxation is learned and, like any learning process, it needs to go through a process of assimilation, accommodation and adaptation, as well as a lot of training and practice.

The final purpose is that it becomes a habit, but with the difference that it is a healthy habit, which produces benefits such as:
- Decrease of muscular tension.
- Decreased heart rate and heart rate intensity.
- Increased arterial vasodilatation and consequently improved peripheral blood flow.
- Decrease in the rhythm, frequency and intensity of breathing.
- Decreased sweating.
- Decrease in adrenaline levels.
- Decrease in cholesterol and fatty acid indices and in general a decrease in sympathetic activity.

6.7.1 Language used in relaxation

When we perform a relaxation, we have to use a language that reaches the unconscious, the message has to be simple, clear, useful and easy to understand. As if we were telling a small child something we want him to understand. It is necessary to repeat the suggestions to find the moment in whichthe person is more receptive with the purpose of automatingthe process. When we eat, when we walk, when we write, these are activities that for the most part are directed by theunconscious, they are learned through repetition, but once learned, a large part of them become automated (we have already talked about this).

Learning to relax is similar to any other type of learning: it consists of a theory and a procedure that must not only be learned and understood, but also felt and believed in, without forgetting that we must practice, practice and practice. The best way to achieve what we propose is to exercise daily, with practice the results will increase.

In the end, the secret to success in any learning process can be summed up in: patience, effort and perseverance.

6.7.2 Semantics and synthesis

The use of gerunds and adverbs provides a guide for the process to flow in such a way that the requests become suggestions, where the person receiving the relaxation is the one who chooses to carry them out. This eliminates possible resistance caused by the desire not to lose control to someoneelse. Some of the gerunds and adverbs most commonly usedin relaxation are the following:

Gerunds:
Breathing, breathing in, observing, experimenting, dis-covering, paying attention, listening, feeling, relaxing, learning, enjoying...

Adverbs:
Calmly, rhythmically, leisurely, comfortably, harmoniously, attentively, slowly, healthily, automatically...

6.7.3 How to improve the effectiveness of suggestions

- Tone of voice appropriate to each message.
- Emphasize keywords.
- Speak with rhythm, pauses and speed appropriate to each message.
- Show confidence and fluency in what is said.
- Short or fractioned suggestions in short sentences.
- Content expressed in positive.
- Repeat them throughout the induction.
- That they are credible.
- Express them with strength and credibility, with emotional involvement.
- Use the descriptions in the different sensory modalities to give them strength and credibility.

6.7.4 Connectors in suggestion escalation

The transition between the phrases must be smooth, without breaking the harmony, the person who is being relaxed must feel that one thing leads to the other in a progressive and natural way, the whole relaxation is a continuum, where suggestions follow one after another and whose realization gives rise to accept the next step willingly. The following connectors should be shown in order of complexity and acceptance, starting with the simplest ones:

  a. **Simple and weak: A and B:** You hear the sound of my voice **and** feel the temperature of your hands on your legs.

  b. **A will allow you to B:** Having your eyes closed **will allow you to** feel the sensations more intensely.

  c. **When A then B: When you** take three deep breaths **then** you will go into even deeper relaxation.

  d. **While A, B: As you** listen to my voice increase your self-confidence.

  e. **As A then B: As you** relax, **then you** will see your breathing become calmer.

  f. **A makes B:** Feeling your body heavier **makes** your whole body relax.

  g. **At the same time as A, B: At the same time that** your conscious mind is attentive to follow the process, your unconscious mind provides you with a state of well-being and tranquility.

6.7.5 Interferences in the relaxation process

During the performance of relaxation, and therefore during the process of internal focusing, the person being relaxed may interfere in achieving the ideal desired state, in order toaddress the problems or objectives of the relaxation. These interferences can be of different nature:

  a. **Conscious:** The progression in relaxation and the physiological and perceptual changes in sensations (feeling of weight, of not being able to move), may provoke, in the person, fear and perception of lack of control over the situation. This could cause the subject to become blocked. To avoid these sensations and not having to stop the relaxation process, the personshould be informed beforehand that he/she is going to feel these sensations, and that it is best to let them happen and amplify, as they are a symptom that the process is developing normally.

b. **Unconscious:** Without realizing it, our mind has gone to past or future thoughts or situations that have nothing to do with what we are pursuing. Above all, they occur during the period of learning relaxation, inthe first few times it is practiced. The mind must be accustomed to the internalization, when this happensand we realize it, we will simply focus on returning tothe internal focus without giving greater importance.

Once the skill of achieving relaxation has been acquired, visualization brings depth to the process.

It is advisable to construct the relaxation taking into account the predominant representational modality of the person to be relaxed. If it is more visual, we will recreate in visual de- tails, if it is auditory, we will take special care in how we use the intonations, the silences and the syllables, we will focus the attention in the sounds, if it is more kinesthetic, we will work with the sensations, with the feelings and the emotions.This makes that some people like to begin the relaxation ac-companied by a quiet background music, or with the sound of the waves, or of a soft rain, or the sounds of spring in thefield. Others like to imagine a wonderful place and recreate themselves in the colors, in the scenery, or they may like to feel that they are walking, doing some activity or just restingand looking at their quiet breathing.

To perform the relaxation, you should look for a comfortable place, ideally, if at first it is done with the body stretched, then get used to perform it in a chair, as this will expand theopportunities to have time and place to carry it out. Make sure that there are no distractions, since in a state of internalfocalization the senses and sounds that would normally go unnoticed are sharpened and these can become distractions.If there is a distracting stimulus (example: a sound), the idealis to incorporate it into the relaxation and make them come to the foreground, in which conscious attention is paid to them, and then use them to relax more deeply (accept and use). For example, if when we are initiating the relaxation, wehear the drill of a neighbor trying to hang a picture, we can introduce in our instructions something like this: *"I want youto imagine that this sound you hear corresponds to a spiral ofrelaxation and as you hear this sound that corresponds to thisspiral... your relaxation will become deeper and deeper".*

We must find out if the person has another phobia, or if thereis something he/she dislikes in order not to introduce it in therelaxation, since it would be activated and it would be very difficult to get him/her to relax properly.

In the same way, it is necessary to ask her in which places she is more relaxed: in the mountains, in the sea, in the cottage, walking with her dog... In this way, the relaxation will be focused on her ideal place to relax. Even so, it is better to use an open language so that the subject can form his visualization and we do not introduce something that is aversive to him. For example, if we are guiding the person through a visualization on the beach and we say: *"You bathe in the seaand when you submerge your head under the water you feela pleasant sensation of well-being".* If this person does not like to feel the sensation of being under the water, we will have broken the harmony, it is possible that he/she will feel uncomfortable and from that moment on he/she will not be able to relax. It would be much better to say: *"You are walking on the beach and maybe you would like to get closer tothe shore and feel the touch of the water on your skin and thus experience sensations that allow you to feel much bet- ter..., or maybe you just want to contemplate the movementof the waves..., how they come and go...".* We are offering you options to choose from.

If the person manifests a symptom of discomfort such as pain, we should not try to deny it, as this will create an interference in the relaxation. We should start by focusing on thatsymptom and even increase it and then make it more bearable. We should never try to suppress the pain completely, because in addition to being in a complex situation, the painmay be fulfilling a warning function (appendicitis). It is important that we teach the person to relax by himself. This is a resource that will give him/her confidence and security. Self-relaxation starts by relaxing the body, adjusting the breathing to a steady rhythm and simply allowing the breathing speed to slow down. Once relaxed, the person can be guided into a deep state of relaxation that will facilitate in- creased receptivity.

During relaxation, the person becomes aware of his or her body. At that point he or she may perceive that his or her body begins to feel heavy or light, warm or cold. Different people have similar sensations, while others experience unusual sensations. When visualizing, most people feel a slight flickering. This Rapid Eye Movement (REM) usually occurs in the same way during sleep in the phase known as REM, this is a normal and natural experience in all people.

There are different relaxation techniques, we will expose some of them that have proven to be very effective. As we have commented previously, once the skill to relax or relax has been acquired, visualization will add depth to the process.

The guide of the content of the relaxation is not something closed, each person can adapt it to the characteristics of the situation and its circumstance.

6.7.6 Relaxation by visualization of a relaxing scene

"Close your eyes..., try to free your mind of thoughts at the same time that you abandon your body to relaxation and free it from tension, for thisit can help you to repeat phrases like: I release thetension of my body, I feel calm, I relax and releasethe muscles, I notice how calmness invades me. Observe how when you inhale you take all the air that your body needs and when you exhale you getrid of everything that is no longer useful...

Imagine that it is a beautiful and sunny spring day..., you are taking a nice walk in the countrysideand you are walking quietly along a path, at the same time that you are leaving behind all the thingsthat bother you and worry you..., you continue walking along that path and you reach a nice and lonelybeach..., and you look at the intense blue of the seaand that makes you perceive a deep calm..., and perhaps there are other shades of color in the water,in the waves, in the environment where you are...,and you contemplate the sky, its brightness, and maybe there are other shades of color in the water,in the waves, in the environment where you are... and you contemplate the sky, its luminosity, and maybe there is a cloud or something that captures your attention and helps you to let go..., you see acomfortable hammock and you lie down placidly onit while you feel its pleasant and warm touch all overyour body..., the contact with the fabric makes yourbody become even heavier and more relaxed..., at the same time you feel very re- laxed...at the same time that you feel very well, you continue breathingslowly and deeply..., and as you breathe in you feelthe fresh breeze, the pleasant aroma of the sea, youfill yourself with energy..., and as you breathe out you free yourself from tension, you immerse your- self in a deeper and deeper state of relaxation..., and perhaps you hear some pleasant sound like the one provoked by the rhythmic coming and going ofthe waves on the shore ,

Now concentrate for a few more moments on what you see, what you hear, what you feel   , this is your special place of relaxation to which you can go whe- never you need it..., repeat to yourself that in this place you feel calm and security, calm, and more strength to face daily difficulties..., continue to en- joy your special place for a few moments...,...,   , repeat to yourself that in this place you feel calm and security, calm, and more strength to face the daily difficulties..., continue enjoying your special place for a few moments...,...,...,... Now, start yourway back with your cells full of energy, with tranquility and se- curity to better face the daily difficulties"...

*I am going to count from 1 a5 and when I reach 5 you will slowly open your eyes and feel a great relax- ation, serenity and tranquility..., 1 enjoy the relaxa- tion..., 2 notice how calmness invades you ,
3 maintain the state of inner peace..., 4 you feel very well, with a great inner strength, 5 open your
eyes slowly   ".*

6.7.7 Self-relaxation (autogenic training)

It is a very short but very effective relaxation, after having practiced the relaxation in the office, we will give instructions for the person to perform it by himself. We work with the sen- sation of weight, breathing and heat, repeating each of these sensations about 6 times. To do this we will use your dominant hand and arm (previously we will have asked you).The purpose is to create an anchorage with the sensation ofweight and to evoke later the sensation of weight, thesensations that we have associated will be felt:

"Put yourself in a comfortable and relaxed position..., rest your hands on top of your legs..., and close your eyes to allow your mind to focus its attention on your breathing and inner sensations , that will make your body start to relax and you will obtain the optimal state of relaxation to get the maximum benefit of what I am going to tell you next....

Feel how when you breathe in you take in everything you need, and feel how your lungs rise and expand to be able to take in all the air that enters through your nose or mouth, whichever iseasier...

Now concentrate on your right hand..., despite having your eyes closed you know perfectly the position of each of your fingers..., and it may seem to you that your hand is motionless..., but whenever there is life there is movement and blood circulates through your hand carrying oxygen to each of its cells..., and you begin to feel how your right hand becomes heavier..., and you can feel the weight of your hand on top of your leg..., and it weighs..., it is as if this great weight on top of your leg and you begin to feel how your right hand becomes heavier..., and you can feel the weight of your hand on top of your leg..., and it weighs..., it is as if that great weight that is on top of your hand prevents itfrom moving..., heavier and heavier..., you can feelhow that sensation of weight extends towards the arm becoming heavier and heavier..., as your handand your leg become heavier and heavier...as yourhand and your right arm becomes heavier, your breathing becomes calmer, softer, you can feel howthe air enters and leaves in a calm and harmoniousway..., it is as if your whole body was breathing, and at the same time, you perceive a sense of calmness and at the same time you perceive a feeling of pleasant warmth in your right hand, and maybe it starts in your fingertips or maybe in the palm of your hand, it is a pleasant warmth, like when we take the sun and we feel its warmth and its energythat fills us , and this makes your whole body relax and you feel very good , and it is the best moment to tell yourself something that you know you wouldlike to do...

Now feel how your arm and your right hand start to feel again the sensation of normal weight while your mind continues to take care of your body..., I will count from 1 to 3 and when you reach 3 you will open your eyes feeling satisfaction and tranquility for your decision..., 1 you feel very well..., 2 your decision is strong and firm..., 3 open your eyessoftly....

6.7.8 Exhibition in imagination

As mentioned in previous pages, in order to overcome a phobia, the sufferer must confront the situation that provokesit, in order to realize that the consequences he or she fears aredispropor-tionate and irrational. It is through experience that, in this case, the negative anchors established between the stimulus and the emotion of fear are broken. Depending on the phobia and the circumstances in which its symptoms manifestthemselves, it may be more or less dangerous to test, in a realway, the per-son's ability to cope with it. There are cases, suchas amax-ophobia (fear of driving) that present an added difficulty and that is that the person who suffers from it is performing a be-havior that involves great danger if it is not executedcorrectly. The subject has in his hands a heavy vehicle, whichcan move at high speeds generating enormous kinetic energy.For this rea-son, the person's first contact with the phobic stimulus must take place in a controlled and safe environment, where there is no fear or real danger to add to his or her ownfear.

It will be through exposure in imagination, both in amaxop-hobia, as in the rest of phobias, where we can make the person visualize effectively the feared events and make them face them with new resources and strategies that they did not have before, first in the form of challenge and later in the form of satisfaction for having achieved their goal: to drive a car with-out suffering the symptoms of anxiety, which until now were manifested by the mere thought of it, or face, in other cases, the dreaded plate of olives, or to enter an elevator ....

It is appropriate to make the exposure gradually and creating emotional distancing, especially when we notice that the per-son finds it very difficult to face the facts. To do this, if neces-sary, we will use the dissociation of the scene. We make the person imagine that he/she is seeing him/herself, suffering the negative events, but he/she sees him/herself on a television screen, movie screen, or something similar. Once the person manifests that he/she feels little or no anxiety, we will asso-ciate him/her again to see him/herself in the phobic scene di-rectly, without any screen to cushion the impact.

The following is an imaginative presentation to illustrate what we have explained. As it is open in its content, it can be used in any case of phobia, although it can be adapted specifically to a particular situation.

The action replay: This exposure in imagination approaches the fear to transform it first into something bearable and then intosomething natural. We will apply it once we verify that the person relaxes and is able to visualize:

"Close your eyes. Try to free your mind of thoughts at the same time that you abandon your body to relaxation and free it of tension, for this it can helpyou to repeat phrases like: I release the tension of my body..., I feel calm..., I relax and release the muscles..., I notice how the calm invades me.

Take three long, deep breaths..., (wait until you take all three breaths).

You can listen to the music (if there is any), the sound of my voice and at the same time feel sensations that come from other senses..., it is curious to observe how, when we have our eyes closed we are able to feel things that normally we do not pay attention to..., observe your breathing...,how when you inhale the air enters through your nose or mouth, your lungs widen and welcome the air to oxygenate your cells..., and perhaps you canfeel the slight tingling of oxygen through your arteries and reaching all your muscles..., and whenyou exhale you release all the tension, all that you no longer need, letting your muscles relax andloosen..., you automatically feel a pleasant sensation of calmness   and as you exhale you free
yourself of all the tension, of everything you no longer need, letting your muscles relax and loosen..., you automatically feel a pleasant sensation of calm..., and you can choose to relax now or do it progressively, experiencing the sensations of tranquility little by little....feel the sensation of the touch of your clothes..., of your hair..., feel the weight of your body in the place where you are..., and how maybe you experience that   your   body   becomes heavier..., or maybe lighter..., or maybe lighter and heavier at the sametime....

Imagine how when you inhale part of that air goes to your arms and descends like a river of clean water flowing down its course between mountains, making life flourish in its path..., and goes to your forearms, and descends to your hands and leaves through your fingertips like a soft breeze....

It is possible that you have areas of your body more relaxed than others..., maybe your right arm and hand are more relaxed than your left arm and hand..., or maybe it is your left arm and hand that is more relaxed than your right arm and hand..., or your forehead..., and your eyelids are more relaxed than your legs..., either way, that doesn't matter now, just like it is possible that your perception of time has changed..., How much time has passed since you are relaxing? 10 minutes..., 20 minutes...

What is the difference between 10 minutes and 2 minutes? or between 15 minutes and 2 hours? Sometimes, if we are impatiently waiting for the bus, 9 minutes may seem like 2 hours..., and othertimes, like when we are watching a good movie or having a nice conversation, 1 hour and a half may seem like 15 minutes..., and quietly allow time to be no impediment to let yourself go to a deeper state of relaxation now or later, because time does not matter now....

Now imagine that you are in the living room of your house, or anywhere where you feel safe and confident..., and you are sitting quietly in your armchair watching TV with the remote control in your hand. You turn on channel 1 and you see yourself in a wonderful place, you are enjoying a well-deserved vacation and you feel great. Recreate yourself with all the details and every time you come back to this channel you will see many more spectacular places. Observe the colors..., the light..., the distance bet-ween you and the objects. Feel the temperature, and possibly you can also feel the air or the breeze if you are outdoors..., or maybe what makes you feel better are the sounds of that place..., a melody..., the song of a bird or the sound of the waves coming and going..., or the sound of the air passing through the leaves of the trees....and you may also perceive smells..., and fragrances..., smells that take us back to pleasant moments..., and maybe you can touch something with your hands and feel its touch, its softness or its texture..., letting the sensations be transmitted through the receptors ofyour fingers, of your skin..., recreate for a few moments of these pleasant sensations...

Now switch to channel 2. In this channel you see yourself just before the feared situation, starting from the first frame in which you have no anxiety or fear yet. And move through the sequence of images until you are in the situation you are afraid of. Notice all the details, the colors..., and the tonalities..., and the light..., and the temperature..., and the sounds..., and your sensation of weight, if you feel light or heavy...

Rate your feeling of discomfort and uneasiness on a scale of 1 a5 (1 no discomfort, 5 very intense discomfort).

Switch to channel 1 (chosen site) you feel again the sensation of security, calm and confidence that this place offers you, look for a comfortable place where you can rest and breathe quietly, without having anything better to do..., and relax quietly in the peace and calm of this place.
Choose one of the objects or people you see in that place, also look at the brightness and tone of their colors.

Change again to channel 2, just before the feared situation (phobic situation) occurs, but this time the object, animal or person that you have taken from channel 1 (chosen site) will also appear on the screen, place it within the scene where you want, try also to change the tone, the brightness of the colors and the characteristics of the feared situationto resemble the stimulus brought from channel 1 where the pleasant situation is projected..., and go forward in the sequence of images until you are in the situation that you fear. Notice all the details, thecolors..., and the tonalities..., and the light..., and the temperature..., and the sounds..., and your sensation of weight, if you feel light or heavy....

What degree of discomfort do you feel from 1 to 5?

Switch back to channel 1 where you feel very well enjoying some very pleasant moments..., observe the details and the sensations you feel..., (chosen place), and choose another object or person you see in that place, and also notice the brightness and to-nality of its colors.

Switch back to channel 2, and stop it at the first frame just before the situation you were avoiding (phobic situation), and when the image is displayed the objects, animals or people you have chosen from channel 1 (chosen site) will also appear on thescreen, and place the one you have just brought intothe scene where you want..., now the situation looks different, and when introducing the second stimulus try to fur-ther adapt the tone and bright- ness of the colors of the phobic situation to resemble the stimuli brought from channel 1.
Reproduces the phobic situation from the first frame to the last with the introduction of the new stimulus (the object, animal or person) ...

Re-evaluate the discomfort from 1 a5...

Switch back to channel 1 where you feel very well enjoying some very pleasant moments..., and ob-serve the details and the sensations you feel (cho-sen place) and choose another object or person you see in that place, and also notice the brightness and tone of its colors.

Switch back to channel 2, which already looks diffe-rent, having adapted it to the 2 previous stimuli, and stop it in the first frame just before the situation you were avoiding (phobic situation), and when theimage is displayed, the objects, animals or people you have chosen from channel 1 (chosen site) will also appear on the screen, and place the one you have just brought into the scene where you want, and when introducing the third stimulus try to furt-her adapt the tone, and the brightness of the colors, and the sounds, and smells or any characteristics ofthe feared situation so that it resembles the stimulibrought from channel 1.

Reproduces the phobic situation from the first frame to the last with the introduction of the new stimulus (the object, animal or person) ...

Re-evaluate the discomfort from 1 a5...

Switch to channel 1 and you are in a safe place, enjoying the feeling of well-being. Recreate yourself with all the details. And observe that place through your five senses, and see what is around you..., and feel the sounds..., and smell the fragrances..., and maybe you might be tasting something..., or maybe feeling the warmth of the sun or the temperature on your skin..., take three deep breaths..., take three deep breaths..., gently close the fist of your right hand and feel how you concentrate on your whole fist gently close the fist of your right hand and feel how you concentrate in your fist all that feeling of tranquility, security and confidence..., open your hand, close it again gently and observe again that feeling of tranquility, security and confidence, open your hand..., and continue relaxing (ancho- ring).

Now switch back to channel 2 (phobic scene). View the movie with the changes you have made by pressing the fast forward button, when you reach the end, rewind to the beginning also in fast forward. How did you feel? Do you feel more or less uneasy? Try now to play the images by pressing the slow-motion button, you can slow down yourself, the ot-hers or both, try it in all ways. What feeling did youhave? Do you have more discomfort or less?

Play the movie of the feared situation with all the changes introduced at the speed you feel most comfortable, it can be: normal, slow or fast speed...

Now put the remote control in your pocket and get into the movie that was being projected, starting from the first sequence to the end, and if at any moment you feel discomfort, close the fist of your right hand and you will feel the sensations of security and self-confidence (we are reinforcing the anchor).

Now go back to your safe place (chosen situation), and take three deep breaths...

I am going to count from 1 a5 and when I reach 5

you will slowly open your eyes and feel a great relax-
ation and tranquility..., 1 enjoy the relaxation..., 2
from now on when you feel uneasiness you can gently
close the fist of your righthand and regain the feeling
of security and confidence..., 3 maintain the state of
inner peace...,
4 you feel very good, start to activate your mus-
cles..., 5 open your eyes slowly".

6.8 Live exhibition

The live exposure represents the final test for the person suffering from phobia. Before arriving here, we have approached
the problem from a safe situation, which offers us the exposure in imagination from a safe place, such as a comfortable
armchair, so that the subject is measured before his fear and
can increase his expectation of overcoming it. We have implemented, through visualization, a behavioral program where
the person experiences the action of driving, or entering an
elevator, or going to a shopping mall..., free of anxiety (PNL).
In addition, we have provided her with a whole series of resources gathered from the Rational Emotive Model(REM) in order to change her false beliefs in relation to the phobia to be
overcome.

Now... the time has come to face fear in a real scenario and
prove that we all have a born winner inside us. As we have
mentioned, both in imaginary exposure and in real exposure,it
is not a good idea to want to move forward too quickly, butlittle
by little, step by step.

It is necessary to try not to abandon the expected state of
tranquility. For this reason, it would be an excellent option to
draw up a list of objectives to be achieved progressively, similar to the one that Wolpe could design[43], from his model of
systematic desensitization, in which it is proposed that the progress in the exposure to fear should be hierarchized, ma-king
a list, for example from 1 to 10, where 1 corresponds tothe
phobic situation of least anxiety and 10 to the maximum.In the
next chapter we will explain, in more detail, how to elaborate
Wolpe's list with a practical example.

What we must have very clear, because it is of **vital impor-**

---

[43] Joseph Wolpe (1915 - 1997). Although he was naturalized in the UnitedStates, he was
born in South Africa. He was a professor of psychiatry at Temple University School of
Medicine in Philadelphia

tance, is that: the first exposures have as a priority objective to maintain the anxiety of the person, who suffers the phobia, in its minimum levels. If we ignore or forget this maxim, we will not be able to advance in the treatment. In these cases, the faster we want to go, the easier it will be to fail. If it is observed that the level of anxiety rises, it is advisable to stop and re-evaluate the steps again, in order to, if necessary, return to previous positions of security. The situations are then returned to and repeated in order to regain confidence and take it from there.

In these cases, if the patient has to be patient, the psychology professional has to show more patience, because the next level is not passed until it is verified that the person feels safe and calm in the level of exposure that is being worked on.

We will try to make all this concrete in a practical example in the next chapter.

"He who learns and learns and does not practice what he knows,is like one who plows and plows and does not sow".
Plato [44]

Chapter 7

7 Case study

This last chapter describes the intervention process of a case of amaxophobia, relating the theoretical content, which has been developed in the previous chapters, with the practice. In this way, the psychology or psychiatry professional, as wellas teachers of road safety training, or anyone interested in knowing more about the diagnostic evaluation process and the treatment of fear of driving or amaxophobia, will be ableto have a holistic view of this problem that is increasingly present in our days. It goes without saying that, although it is not strictly necessary to have read the theory in depth, it is obvious that understanding the theoretical foundation facilitates the application of the techniques and resources that have been described throughout this book.

From here, if you wish, we will develop, from a practical point of view, a clinical picture from beginning to end.

7.1 Case Study secondary amaxophobia

7.1.1 Sandra is afraid of driving on the highways

First session (60 minutes)

Objective of the session: To obtain as much information about the case as possible and to establish a diagnostic evaluation.

Diagnostic evaluation of Sandra's amaxophobia

---

[44] Plato (427 - 347 B.C.) Born in Athens. Greek philosopher, pupil of Socrates. Author of works such as: The Banquet, The Republic, Plato's Dialogues

In this first session we meet Sandra, she is 24 years old, sheis a primary school teacher and drives her car daily to go from home to the school where she works and then back home. Since she had a scare entering a freeway, she looks for any way to go places avoiding entering freeways, highways or similar roads.

a. Individual interview with Sandra

- Following the protocol of the interview technique, explained in chapter 3, we came to know that Sandra obtained her driving license at the age of 18, forced by circumstances, since to go to the University (Sandra was starting her degree in Primary Education at the Autonomous University of Barcelona) the combination of public transport was chimerical, as she needed almost three hours each way, when in a private vehicle the itinerary could be done, calmly, in 45 minutes.

- He had no problems in the theoretical training and, although he had some difficulty in the driving test, he finally obtained his driving license after a few hours of practice, dedication and effort.

- He immediately began to drive, as the public transport route was an ordeal. After obtaining her driving license, she spent a period of "normality", approximately six years, which helped her to gain confidence and skill in driving. She had taken a liking to driving without beinga slave to schedules, nor to endless waiting at train or bus stops...

- Everything was great, until one day, when she was on her way to a primary school in Vallés Oriental, to make her first substitution as a teacher in charge of a primary school classroom..., she got (according to her) the scare of her life. During the trip, when she was about to join the B-224 road to the A-P7 highway, without knowing how, she was about to collide sideways with atruck. Even today, he still can't understand what hap- pened... In his own words: *"Maybe because my head was stressed thinking about how I would do with my first students. Maybe it was because I had been in a week full of anxiety because, since I and my partner decided to live together, the relationship began tocrumble, as if it were a bridge whose supporting pillars had been removed... This whole situation generated a lot of stress and anxiety... The thing is that I still feel the beeping of the truck, as if it were a locomotive without brakes announcing that it was going to crush me against the asphalt...".*

- *He* goes on to tell me: *"(...) It was at that moment thatI began to feel my heart racing, to the point that I thought it would never beat at a normal rate again. In a moment my clothes were completely soaked with sweat and my stomach felt as if a hand was squeezingit with all its might..."*

- Although Sandra avoided the collision, she could not get away from her anxious thoughts that she could have died at that moment, nor (and this worries her even more) could she or knew how to manage the symptomsof anxiety she was suffering, on the contrary, it seemsthat they were increasing, because she could not see how to stop on the shoulder, she thought that if she didso she would put herself in serious danger. Thinking that he would suffer a heart attack at any moment, hesaw an information panel indicating that the Montseny area was 500 meters away. She continues in the right lane at an abnormally slow speed, as she feels like sheis in a cloud (pure anxiety). Trucks and buses overtakeher, expressing their complaint with loud and longbeeps. The few meters left to get out of the abyss, where she feels immersed, become endless... Finally, she is safe! With her vehicle stopped at the service area, she calls her friend Carol to come to her rescue, not daring to call anyone else. She dies of embarrass- ment just thinking of a plausible excuse for them to come and get her... Only Carol can understand her, asshe knows very well what anxiety is (Carol had over- come a few months ago an agoraphobia disorder).

- After a few minutes - although she can't tell if it was hours or minutes - she admits that she is not able to go on, not even to start the car's engine. She dials the number of her friend Carol on her cell phone and asks her in a broken and sobbing voice to come and pick herup (...).

- Since that episode, every time she has to take a route that involves passing through a stretch, even a short one, of highway or freeway, she avoids it because, when she has tried it, she has always ended up in a panic crisis. On occasions, she has even become anxious at the mere thought of having to travel on a freeway.

- With Carol she will share all the experience she has just lived, but she does not dare to talk about it with other friends, perhaps for fear that they will see her as a *"freak"* or think she is *"crazy", she does not want to say anything to her parents either,* because she thinks it will make them suffer..., and with her partner even less, because he is capable of gloating and mocking her weakness.

- On the day of our interview, he says he is weighing the possibility of giving up driving, although he knows that such a decision will influence too many aspects of his life, but right now he believes there is no solution.

b. CEMIC Administration (2). Secondary Amaxophobia

- The administration and tabulation of the questionnaire gives us the following data: the total score of the questionnaire is 54, so that according to the interpretation and intervention criteria of the CEMIC (1 and 2), expressed in previous pages, Sandra is located in Level 5 of amaxophobia, High level, so we can consider that we are dealing with a clear case of manifest fear of driving.

- Homework: Before finishing the session, I ask Sandra to read some photocopies that I give her, which explain how to carry out the Rational Emotive Model (REM) Paradigm A-B-C-D-E (plus F) Thinking Debate, by Ellis and Grieger (2003), described in the theoretical block. I tell him "If you read it, it will be easier and more effective the next session, because we will work on the model that you will find in this document that I give you".

7.1.2 Applying the A-B-C-C-D-E-F paradigm to Sandra's case

Second session (60 minutes)

Objective of the session: To teach Sandra to be aware of her negative, irrational and illogical thoughts and to change them for more positive and rational ones.

A. Activating experience:

From the summary of the interview, it can be easily extracted that Sandra's amaxophobia triggering experience is:

The moment when she was on her way to the kindergarten and primary school and was about to get on the highway, she suddenly found a truck bearing down on her. Let's not forget that it was her first job and that in recent weeks her relationship with her partner had kept her in an extreme and continuous state of anxiety.

B. Thoughts and beliefs:

The illogical, or irrational, thoughts running through Sandra's mind after the freeway event: P1 *"The free- way is an extremely dangerous road that I have to avoid"*; P2 *"My heart is going so fast that it will literallyexplode"*; P3 *"If I don't go at least 120 on the freewayI am a risk to myself and others"*; P4. *"Only to me do these weird things happen"*. These unrealistic thoughtsgive way to...

C. Consequences of thoughts:

The thoughts of the previous phase increase Sandra's fear of driving on highways or similar and make her feel like a fragile and useless person. Just the thought of entering the highway provokes in her symptoms of anxiety (sweating and accelerated heart rate), so her anxiety feeds her fear, thus creating the circular situation of "Fear of feeling Fear". Hence, Sandra flees or avoids entering fast lanes, with acceleration lanes and with more than one lane for each direction.

D. Discussion of thoughts:

Negative thought P1: "The highway is an extremely dangerous road to avoid. Sandra should know that freeways are the safest roads in the road network. Statistically, they are where the fewest accidents occur. Although it is true that, although the probability of accidents is lower than on other roads, when they do occur, they are usually serious (due to the high speed at which people drive on these roads). In other words, there are fewer deaths on freeways than on other interurban roads.

- Negative thought P2: *"My heart is going so fast thatit will literally explode".* Fortunately, a healthy heart, especially if it is that of a young person, is designed to change its rhythm without any problem.Think of the heart rate you can reach when you gorunning because you see that you are going to missthe bus... Or when you climb a flight of stairs a littlefaster than usual... You will agree with me that, in similar cases, if we had a heart rate monitor, the reading would be closer to 150 beats than to 60 beats of heart rate. So, it is a false belief to think that a young and healthy heart can burst because we notice, at a certain moment, that it is accelerating... Many more times than we think it accelerates, without us being aware of it, and nothing hap-pens.

- Negative thought P3: *"If I don't go at least 120 km/h on the highway, I am a risk to myself and ot-hers".* Perhaps a review of the General Traffic Regulations would clarify the doubt (for Sandra and possibly for many drivers) that the speed of 120 km/hour is the generic maximum speed establishedfor this type of road. It also seems that few driversare aware that the generic minimum speed on highways is 60 km/hour. This being so, although itmay seem an ab-erration to some, a car driving in the right lane of a highway at 70 or 80 km/hour is doing so correctly. So, it should not be a problem if someone decides to drive at a cruising speed (I in-sist in the right lane) of 80 km/hour. Probably the real danger is in the multitude of drivers who, apparently, believe that the generic minimum speed on highways and freeways is 120 km. That being the case, Sandra should not worry about what ot- hers might think of her. If she doesn't feel like speeding at more than 80 km/hour, she can ride in herright lane. Hour, in her right lane, for whatever reason, it is her right and she should not feel bad about it.

- Negative thought P4: *"Only to me these strange things happen".* Unfortunately, an increasing num-ber of people suffer from phobias. Phobias to olives, to clothes with buttons, to elevators, to closed spa-ces, etc., etc., etc. In some cases, it is more common to say that you suffer from them. There are many people who say without problems that they suffer from claustrophobia, or that they are afraid of heights? Perhaps it is not so common to hear that

136

someone suffers from amaxophobia, or more specifically, that they are afraid of driving only if they are on the highway. But be that as it may, it is one more phobia that has no greater or lesser prognosis or lesser or greater prominence than the others. Suffering from this or any other phobia should not put us in a very poor situation of inferiority or of thinking that we are weirder than a green dog.

At the end of this phase, Sandra should have changed her irrational, negative, illogical thoughts for others that make her feel calm, peaceful and secure. In this way she will regain her self-esteem and be back on the road to overcoming her amaxophobia.

E. Final result:

We found that, after having discussed the thoughts in phase "D", Sandra's level of distress and discomfort de-creased. The discouragement and worry scores that were high in phase C (Consequences of the thought) have decreased.

F. Learning from experience:

We tell Sandra that, at the end of the day, when she is in bed, before going to sleep, she should review the whole process from phase "A" to "E". How she has been aware of the activating experience (A), how she has "hunted" her negative thoughts (B), how those negative thoughts have generated the feeling of helpless- ness, accompanied by insecurity, and how the ThoughtDebate (D) has transformed the negative ideas into much more neutral or more positive thoughts, to finally be able to verify that the result (E) confirms that her level of emotional discomfort has been reduced.

7.1.3 Exposure by visualization and imagination Third session (60 to 90 minutes)

Objective of the session: To expose Sandra to her fear through the technique of visualization in imagination.

Following some of the techniques described in the previous chapters and, once we have agreed on the imaginary place where Sandra tells us that she can enjoy calm, peace, and security, etc. And, being in a comfortable place, free (if possible) of distracting noises, and other external interruptions... We start the relaxation (see previous chapters). Once Sandrais relaxed, with her eyes closed and following our voice we say to her:

- Us. "I want you to visualize a paradisiacal beach, it is a warm day in early summer, and you are enjoying the sun, and the sound of the sea and the peace that this place gives you....and you are beginning to feel the tranquility of lying down..., resting your body on a hammock..., andas you listen to the soft sound of the waves..., you beginto feel a deep relaxation..., and when the waves gently approach, they make your relaxation even deeper..., andbeing in that place you feel how calm and peace invade you and that makes you feel good..., perfectly good..., calm and re- laxed..., calm and relaxed......, calm and re- laxed..., you feel good..., very good..., so good that you could face anything..., it is possible that you feel how theenergy of the sun strengthens all the particles of your body, and that makes you feel more and more..., re- laxed..., your mind is in peace..., your body is very..., very relaxed..., it has been a long time since you felt thisfeeling of peace and tranquility..., and .I am going to askyour unconscious to remember that from now on every time I tell you "**I want you to relax, go back to the beach**"..., you will visualize again the beach where you are now and you will enter in this state of peace and tranquility and you will feel well..., perfectly well..." (we re- peat the same thing).(we repeat the anchor)..., "I am going to ask your unconscious to re- member that..., from now on..., every time I say to you "**I want you to relax,go back to the beach**"..., you will en- ter again in this state of peace and tranquility and you will feel well..., perfectly well...". At this point we could have used any otherkind of anchor.

From here we observe that Sandra is in an intermediate state of relaxation, we continue forward because it is not necessary to reach a very deep level to achieve a good visualization. In any case, if it is considered that she has not reached the de- sired degree of relaxation, we would continue to insist with phrases related to the situation or the context of relaxation chosen by the person. Once we have achieved that Sandra's unconscious associates (anchors) the phrase of:

> "***I want you to relax, go back to the beach...,***
> *you will get back into this state of peace and tran-*
> *quility and you will feel good..., perfectly good".*

We proceeded to confront the person with his or her phobic stimulus. In Sandra's case, this was done as follows...

- We. Well Sandra..., now I am going to count from one to three, and when I get to three, or maybe before I get to three..., you will start to visualize..., or maybe hear, or feel..., sensations related to your fear of driving   , I want you to go..., at the same time that I am going to count forward..., to the moment..., to the day you were going to Vallés Oriental..., to your first day of work as a teacher...at the same time that I am going to count for- ward..., to the moment..., to the day you were going to Vallés Oriental..., to your first day of work as a teacher.

   I want you to imagine that you are near the entrance to the A-P highway..., you are driving and thinking about how you are going to get there   you are driving and thin-
   king about how the school will be, how your colleagues will be, how the children you will teach will be..., you area bit nervous because of the unknown situation you are going to face, you also feel some anxiety because you don't see continuity in your relationship...you count for- ward..., one..., images appear..., sounds..., 2..., it is possible that you are feeling those symptoms, 3..., suddenly you hear the thunderous beep of a truck that has appeared out of nowhere. Curiously, your heart, although it accelerates, does not accelerate as much as you remembered, and you also notice that yourhands are sweating, but much less than you expected"

We let a few seconds pass and continue...

- We. Okay Sandra, I want you to continue with your eyes closed and staying more or less in the position you are in,I would like you to tell me what is happening....

- *Sandra: I am in the acceleration lane   I am going to join the highway, I feel a little nervous because I don't know if I will be competent enough to face the challenge of being the teacher of children who are no more than 8 years old. I also feel the weight of the failure of my relationship..., that distresses me. I am already merging intothe right lane of the highway, I have looked in the rear- view mirror and the road is clear..., Suddenly... Noooooooo!*

We observe that Sandra moves restlessly in the armchair, shaking her head from left to right and repeating No! No!

- We: what is happening?

- *Sandra: a truck was about to hit me..., I didn't see it..., I don't know where it came from..., I didn't see it; I didn't see it..., my heart was racing and I feel the sweat on my hands and clothes and a knot in my stomach, but it's funny, everything is much milder than I remembered. It'sas if the symptoms have lessened.*

Sandra's face now shows an expression somewhere between disbelief and some discomfort.

- Us: move on a little bit What happens after the initial scare?

- *Sandra: the situation has surprised and upset me, I want to get off the highway..., I can't..., I want to stop on the shoulder..., I can't either, I feel I'm in a very dangerous place, I'm somewhat blocked, I must be extremely cautious..., I slow down..., I dare not go over 70 km. per hour..., trucks and buses overtake me and honk at me, my heart is still beating fast....*

He keeps moving around in the armchair as if he hasn't quite found a comfortable position.

- We: Sandra continues.

- *Sandra: finally, I see my salvation..., a sign tells me thatI am just a few minutes away from a service area..., it seems that the pain in my stomach loosens a little, my heart rate normalizes, and I hardly notice the sweat.*

- We: very well Sandra continues a little bit more.

- I am already in the service area, the car is parked well...,I feel bad, I do not see myself able to get out of this situation without help, but I do not want to call my pa- rents..., and less my partner..., I call my friend Carol, shewill be able to help me.

In this first exposure in imagination Sandra has already decreased her symptoms... Good! We continue.

- We: Okay Sandra, I am going to free you from that situation so annoying for you, I am going to count down from3 to 1, so that you return to the beach, to that place of calm and security... 3 you start to feel, again the sound of the waves as they reach the beach to then recede backto the sea and then, as in an endless loop they return again to the shore..., that soft i rhythmic sound makes you deepen in that state of relaxation and peace. 2..., Atthe same time you can visualize in the distance, in the horizon line, how the turquoise blue of the sea merges with the light blue of the sky..., some white clouds scattered like little pieces of cotton that sway in that blue firmament..., and 1..., **I want you to relax, go back to the beach...,** that's Sandra..., I want you to enjoy that calm, that peace and, that tranquility that this beach givesyou. It is as if that place transmits you all its energy..., the strength of the sea, the sun, the earth, the sea breeze..., you are receiving all that energy now... that is..., you feel more relaxed, more confident, stronger..., Iwant you to enjoy that feeling..., I want you to be awareof your state of relaxation, of the calm and serenity you are experiencing now..., that is, very good..., you are doing very well Sandra.

We notice that Sandra's face reflects all the calm and tranquility she is feeling, imagining and experiencing in that ideal seascape.

- We: Now that you are aware of your situation of calm, peace, tranquility, security and strength..., I want you to maintain that state in which you find yourself now and..., on the count of 1 to 3 visualize yourself again starting from the moment before you had the mishap with the truck, until Carol came to pick you up at the service area,but..., remember that this time you will have all the energy, all the strength and all the security that the beach transmits to you Remember that this time you will have all the energy, all the strength and all the security that the beach transmits to you... I would like that this time, on the count of three, you visualize for yourself the whole sequence that I have described. So..., 1... You are about to enter the highway..., 2..., you are in the acceleration lane..., 3..., Visualize the whole sequence and when you get to the point where your friend Carol comes to pick you up tell me NOW! From then on, I will keep asking you questions and you will answer me by keeping your eyes closed and staying more or less in the position you are in at the moment.

Sandra has already been immersed in her imagination for a few seconds. However, this time she shows hardly any agitation. Her face, although not totally serene, does not reflect the restlessness of the first visualization... She seems to be calmer than the previous time. We know that she is visualizing, because her pupils do not stop still, we can perceive theeye movement through her eyelids, they are the same RapidEye Movements that our eyes do when we are dreaming (REMphase in English or REM in Spanish). After a few minutes thatseem like an eternity... Sandra barely opens her mouth to whisper..., YA!

- We: how did you feel this second time?

- *Sandra: better, it's as if what was happening wasn't with me...*

- We: okay, I am glad, that means that your mind is opening to other ways of facing the situation, maybe with more security, maybe with more tranquility..., I am going to count down from 3 to 1 and when I get to 1, or maybe before, you will be back on the beach... 3 you are going back to that calm beach..., 2 it is easy for your mind to go back to that place of calm and peace... 1 **I want youto relax, go back to the beach.**

Soon we see how Sandra enters a deeper relaxation, her face now shows full serenity, her breathing is regular, slow and deep. It seems as if her body has become leaden.

- Us: Well Sandra, enjoy that peace..., let the energy of that place strengthen your body and mind..., that's it..., you are doing very well..., you feel so well that you fall deeply asleep on that comfortable hammock and as you
well know, when we fall deeply asleep, we dream..., and I want you to dream that you wake up one morning, but not now, but two years ago, you are two years younger, exactly 22..., at that time everything was going well..., you are calm, strong and confident... That is, look...You are 22 years old and curiously you see yourself in similarsituations to the day you met the truck..., you even see yourself making the same entrance, you are close to the highway, right in the acceleration lane, where you find yourself in a similar situation to the other day..., but lookhow you react...But look at how you reacted two years ago, everything is just a simple scare, a warning that youhave to be more attentive in your driving, you immediately recover and continue at a good pace along thehighway..., that's it, that's how you faced these situationstwo years ago. Very good, you are doing very well...

    Now..., **I want you to relax, go back to being on the beach...,** that is you are in that wonderful place and immediately you feel that your mind and your body are filled with strength and security and, to that is going to be added your way of facing driving the way you did two years ago. And, being aware of all that strength..., I will count to three and when you get to three, or maybe before, youwill visualize again the scenario in which you had that scare

with the truck, but this time you will face it in the same way you would have faced it two years ago..., it is nothing new for you, because that was your highway driving response program, your mind knows it well, it only has to use that response style again Visualize the whole
sequence from beginning to end, although, if you want, you can change that end..., maybe when you get to the service area you want to continue to the destination you had initially set, just as you would have done two, three or four years ago... When you finish, tell me Now!

The idea is that Sandra can see herself going through this traumatic situation without feeling fear or anxiety and that her feeling is not one of panic or terror, but a neutral feeling. We are reprogramming, in a progressive way (through several visualizations followed by the same sequence), her way of perceiving and feeling the situation.

After a short but endless time, Sandra says YA!

- We: Very well Sandra..., how are you feeling?
- *Sandra. The truth is that I have felt pretty good, I don't know, it's as if every time I visualize it I feel more confident and calm.*
- Us: What have you visualized?

- *Sandra. It's very funny, because when the truck honked at me, I reacted as I would have done two years ago, I thought, "Hey, asshole, let's see if you don't abuse the little ones". I got a little scared and my heart skipped a beat, but at no time did I see myself sweating or my stomach in a fist.*
- We: All right, continue?
- *Sandra. The surprise was that I didn't want to stop at the service area, I continued on to my destination....*
- Us: How did you feel when you got to the place where you wanted to go in the first place?
- *Sandra, Buahhh! I felt great... I feel great!*
- We: Very good Sandra, now I'm going to ask you simply to go back to the beach 1.., 2..., 3 **I want you to relax, go back to the beach.**

We are going to take Sandra out of relaxation. It is always convenient to bring the person out of relaxation from a calm and serene situation, because this state of calm and serenity

143

is the one that will remain after the session. Once she has spent a few seconds visualizing herself on the beach...

- We: Now Sandra I will count from 1 to 4 and when I reach4 you will come out of the relaxation feeling very good,
  you will feel as if you had taken one of those naps that feel so good, a restorative nap... Everything you have visualized will be fixed in your memory, both conscious andunconscious and will become your new functioning program.... From now on you will face you're driving on the highways in the same way as you did when you were 22 years old, even better, if possible, because you will feel all the strength and security that you felt on the beach Now
  I count to four and you come out of the relaxation feeling very well..., 1 you feel the energy running through your arms..., 2 you feel how your legs recover mobility and strength..., 3 you feel how your whole body recovers all its energy..., that's it..., 4 you can slowly open your eyes...

As Sandra gradually comes out of relaxation and wakes up, as if she had just woken up from a nap, we ask her "How didit go?" "Was it easy to visualize?" "What did you think of the experience?". We take the opportunity to tell him that next time he will go into relaxation faster and deeper. We keep telling her, "You will see that next time, as soon as you settle into the chair, you will enter into a much deeper relaxation than today. She does not know it, but we are suggesting to her unconscious that in the next session she will enter into relaxation immediately.

7.1.4 Self-relaxation and self-reprogramming exercise

We tell Sandra to practice the technique that we have just carried out of exposure by visualization in imagination. The idea is for Sandra to become familiar with it for two reasons:
a) on the one hand, if she practices it often, she will reinforce the program we have worked on today and, on the other hand,
b) if she masters it, she will be able to use the technique to reprogram any experience that causes her pain, dis- tress or discomfort. Through visualization, you can reexperience, interpret and feel the moment you have lived, in a calmer and more peaceful way. The final visualization must be neutral and free of any variable that causes you to feel fear. We want unwanted cognitive and physical symptoms tobe eliminated. You have to visualize the experience and re- view it, until you integrate it as an everyday situation, as onemore routine, that we encounter and resolve without major importance and that leaves no

trace in our daily work.

7.1.5   Live exhibition

Fourth session (90 to 120 minutes)

Objective of the session: To reinforce the first part of confrontation by visualization in imagination. To expose Sandra, live to her fear in real traffic on the highway.

We started the session in the office of the CFORP training and psychology center. Sandra comes in beaming, looking more relaxed than in previous sessions. To my question "How have these two weeks been?" (Sandra called to cancel the previous visit), she answers me... *"Sorry I couldn't attend last week, but I have some good news to give you..., the day after I left here Pau (my ex-partner), told me that the best thing is that we separate our ways, because he had realized that I was right and the only thing we were achieving is to hurt each other... I was a couple of days quite bad and with some anxiety. I listened to you and visualized several times how my life would be a year from now with him or without him, following the visualization technique we did here last time. And, without realizing it, the anxiety has been diluting..., and now, although it seems that in some moments I feel like a failure, deep down I feel calm, because it was very clear to me that our relationship had no future".*

> One of the variables that can determine the success or failure of our intervention is directly related to the possibility that the amaxophobic person is exposed to an external source of anxiety, as in the case of Sandra or Manel. Other extreme situations such as suffering from harassment at work, or psychological abuse, etc., that feed a high state of anxiety will make it impossible for us to make progress in the treatment.

Sandra has just given me the best news I could receive from her, not because I am happy about her breakup with Pau, because it neither benefits nor harms me personally, but I am happy to see that she is involved in the treatment, because that will undoubtedly benefit the process of overcoming her phobia.

- We: I am glad to see that your new situation makes you calmer. I also see that you have practiced self-relaxation and the visualization technique in imagination. I congratulate you.

Sandra keeps telling me how well the self-relaxation exercises have helped her not only to visualize herself driving on the freeway, but also to see what her new single life is going to be like.

- We: Okay, I think it's great that you have transferred that learning to other aspects of your life. If you like, let's move on to the visualization session. You will see that assoon as you sit on the chair, your body and mind, which have memory of the experience of the previous time, willimmediately enter into a deeper relaxation.

- *Sandra: Ah, how nice!*

Before starting the visualization technique in imagination, I describe to Sandra what the objectives of the session are, butI don't tell her that today we are going to end up doing a live show, a real show with her driving down the highway.

In the visualization we have reviewed and reinforced what we worked on in the previous session. We have incorporated the fact that Sandra can see herself driving in the center lane, because today she told me that she is afraid of being trapped between two rows of cars on her right and left (this is a very common situation in people who suffer from amaxophobia).

When we finish the visualization in imagination, after asking the usual questions: How did you feel? Did you have any difficulties? Etc. I tell Sandra...

- We: Come on! We're leaving.

Sandra's face is pure surprise, she tells me all the time "We're leaving! Where are we going? I tell her I want to see how she drives. While I'm telling her all this, I'm taking my car keys, opening the door and inviting Sandra to get out.

The strategy is not to give Sandra time for her thoughts to feed her fear and by extension her anxiety. So, before she knows it, she's already sitting in the driver's seat adjusting her seat.

> *Before moving on to the live exposition, let me tell you that in my case I am a psychologist and a teacher of road training, so that, in real expositions in traffic open to traffic in general, I have solved the problem of accompanying the person who suffers from amaxophobia. If this were not the case, we would have to resort to another formula that I will explain in the closing chapter of the book.*

Having said that, let's move on to Sandra's live exhibition...

- *Sandra. Ah, well! But... You're not going to put me on the freeway? No?*

- We: For the moment my intention is to watch you drive. Come on! When you're ready: seat, seat belt, mirrors, etc. we start off and turn the first street to the left.

Sandra drives with ease, at first, she looks a little nervous. We've been driving around Viladecans for about 15 minutes, she doesn't know the town, so she doesn't suspect that two more turns to the left and one to the right take us straight to the acceleration lane to enter the C-32 highway. I still don't know in which exit we are going to leave..., everything will depend on how Sandra reacts.

- We: Very good Sandra, I see that you control my little Suzuki very well. We will turn left..., that's it..., then left again and then immediately right....

Sandra is facing the car in a straight line, after her last right turn, when she sees the blue sign indicating the option to enter the C-32... She immediately says to me...

- *Sandra... Oh, my God! The sign tells me to take the C-32. You don't expect me to get in?*

- We: I don't know, what do you say? While we're at it! Anyway, the next exit is less than 2 km away... Shall we go in?

- *Sandra. Come on! Let's go in.*

The small utility vehicle, equipped with double pedals and mirrors (it is a driving school vehicle) heads for the beginning of the acceleration lane. I can notice how Sandra is concentrating..., I see her looking through the outside left mirror, Ialso look through my complementary mirror... On the right lane a small delivery truck is approaching..., I see how, whileputting the left turn signal, it moves progressively to facilitatethe incorporation... Sandra enters without problems. I can hear how she has just exhaled a deep breath, as if she had held her breath longer than she should.

Before her unconscious decides for her whether she is going to show joy, fear, or anxiety for the small feat she has just achieved (getting onto the highway with little anxiety). I, rather quickly, so as not to give her the option to think or feel about what we are really doing (driving on the highway), tell her....

- We: Do you know that you could have been a student of mine at the Autonomous University of Barcelona? If you had done the degree of Pedagogy, or the Master ofPsych

147

pedagogy we would have coincided in some class. By the way, how is it that you repeated the fourth year of your degree 3 times?

This situation that I have just invented will provoke a sufficiently strong feeling in Sandra, to displace a possible outburst of fear that may occur at this moment when she is facing her phobia. Let's not forget that she has just faced, out of the blue[45], the activating experience that triggered her fear...

- *Sandra, I don't know where did you get the idea that I failed three times in the fourth year of my degree?*

She looks uncomfortable, breathing a little faster than normal, but the cause of her discomfort is not that we are driving on the C-32, but because she is angry...

- *Sandra. I don't understand why you're telling me that I was a bad student....*

As we continue to move forward in the right lane, although she is attentive to the traffic situation, it seems as if Sandra is driving on automatic... We are traveling at a speed of 90 km/hour. It's as if she's comfortable with the driving, but tremendously annoyed by what I'm telling her.

- Us: Well, I've only seen it on your transcript. But we're not going to argue about that. I'd probably get confused looking at your reports.

Sandra's face is red as a tomato, I would say it expresses anger. I think I am getting what I want. The emotion of anger stops and prevents the possibility that fear can manifest itself, because one emotion can block the appearance of another. It is very rare for a person, for example, to be sad and happy at the same time, or to express anger while showing tenderness.

Sandra has not noticed, but we have already passed the exit where we were supposed to leave. The situation is tense and uncomfortable... When we are just a few meters away from exhausting the possibility of exiting the C-32 before going straight into the Garraf tunnels, I tell Sandra.

- We: You have every reason, and every reason, to be angry with me. In fact, you may be even angrier when you find out that everything, I have told you is a figment of my imagination because, although it is true that I am a teacher

---

[45] Although, the wording of the sentence may make it seem that we have for-ced the situation without previous preparation, it is not true since before the real exposure we have worked on the phobic situation in visualization by imagination.

Sebastián Sánchez Marín

at UAB, we teachers are not in the business of snooping on students' academic records. Teachers are notin the business of snooping on students' academic re- cords, especially not those of students who are not our own because, among other reasons, we do not have access to them. I have only done this so that you could seethat we have been driving along the highway for quite a while and that at no time have you shown, nor do you show, signs of fear or anxiety... Maybe a little angry, butnothing more.

Sandra looks at me with eyes of disbelief and, with a half-smile, tells me (verbatim) *"You're a real scumbag"*. Her half-smile has turned into laughter....

- We: Do we continue through the tunnels until we reach Sitges or do we leave at this exit?

- *Sandra: No! We leave here, the tunnels cost a lot of money and we have to save for the Master's degree I'm planning to take in Psych pedagogy at the UAB (she smiles again).*

We return by the inland road, I'm sure we could have returned by the C-32 highway, but I remember my own advice and decide not to force. It is clear to me that Sandra is going to leave today knowing she is a winner. I want to give her a boost of self-esteem...

Before moving on to the autonomous exposure, we do two more 60-minute sessions drive on all the nearby highways,entering and exiting the coastal beltway, the C-32, the C-31(all highways). We continue to insist that he continues to practice self-relaxation at home and that he visualizes himselfdriving on all the highways and freeways that he had driven on before "D" day. We continue to reinforce her successes and minimize any moments of doubt or "Ouch! Until, just likewhen we put her in the car the first time, out of the blue...

Today, when Sandra goes to get into our Suzuki, we ask her "Where is your car? She answers, *"In the back street"*. Ok, we answer her. Go and look for it and we will wait for you here...

I want you to follow me with your car.

7.1.6 Autonomous exposure

Both Sandra's car and mine have a Bluetooth hands-free phone system. Before leaving, I tell her that I am going to make a call so that we can stay connected for the duration of the autonomous exhibition. If the need does not arise, we will not use this means of communication.

Sandra follows me... I'm going towards the C-32, my intention is to do the same route we did the first day of live exhibition: enter the C-32 in Viladecans and exit in Castelldefels just before the tunnels, only this time we will exit to rejoin and return by the same highway to Viladecans.

During the trip we have been going at a speed between 80 and 100 km per hour. Sandra follows me, even when I over-take a truck.

Halfway through the outward journey, I ask Sandra, "Everything OK? And she answers me *"Everything OK... Do you have any problems? Didn't we agree that we were only going to talk if there were any complications?* Her good mood makes me think that everything is really OK. I feel happy.

When we are back, in our center, I tell Sandra how happy I am to see how she has overcome all her fears, I tell her that she is a real champion and that now I hope she will return home wherever she wants... If she likes to use a stretch of highway, great! But if she decides to go by road that's fine too. I tell her "Now that you know how phobias and anxiety work..., you decide". I give him that message because I know he's going to face his fear....

Two weeks later, when I think that maybe Sandra's return home did not go as well as I expected, Lourdes (the secretary of CFORP) calls me to show me a photo that has just arrived from Sandra to our WhatsApp, in it you can see Sandra with her car next to a sign indicating the entrance to the village where you can read "Sant Feliu de Guíxols". At the bottom of the photo the message says "Hi guys, here I am in Sant Feliu... All the way on the highway... You are Cracs! The message is followed by several emoticons with happy faces.

7.1.7 Final evaluation

We ask Sandra (as in all the cases we have dealt with) to come and see us, as she has to answer the CEMIC 2 questionnaire again, so that we can establish a numerical comparison between before and after our intervention.[46]

7.1.8 Observations of the practical sessions

---

[46] Sandra was part of our study, published in Securitas Vialis, on the "Evaluation of the effectiveness of a program designed to overcome the fear of driving or amaxophobia", referenced in previous pages.

As it is to be expected, not all people react in the same way to treatments, just as not all people, when a teaching-learning process is established, learn at the same pace. The sessions that Sandra did were enough to overcome her fear of driving, and although they can be a point of reference, it mustbe assumed that the review is indicative. Thus, it is reasonable to think that another person may need one or more sessions more, or less, for the exposure in imagination, or need more, or less time, or more reinforcement in the exposure ofthe actual accompanied practice or in the autonomous expo-sure. Forcing the pace so that the person advances without having matured in his struggle to overcome fear, or in his learning process, can be the cause of a resounding failure. The ideal situation is to adapt to the pace of assimilation andlearning of the person who wants to overcome his fear of driving. Only in this way and using correctly and in a structuredway, the techniques described can we help people who havetrusted us, to successfully overcome their amaxophobia.

Similarly, during the internship, the trainer must make it a priority to monitor the anxiety level of the trainee. If anxietygets out of control, learning slows down or is cancelled. It is of vital importance that the student finishes the practice without anxiety, that each session ends with the feeling thathe has advanced not only in learning, but also in his fight against his fear of driving.

Chapter 8

Closing

Before concluding this book, I would like to take a position on a professional controversy that I observe is occurring as amaxophobia becomes more socially visible. It has to do withthe live exposure phase in secondary amaxophobia (people with driving experience) and; with the teaching-learning process for obtaining a driving license for people who suffer (without ever having driven) from amaxophobia.

It is obvious that the live exposure (actual exposure) of amaxophobia is nothing like that of any other phobia. In previous pages we have described the difference between expo-sing someone to their phobia, for example, of using elevatorsand that of exposing an amaxophobic to their fear (their phobia) of driving on the freeway, or in any other situation related to the fear of driving. In the first case, if the experience does not go well, the risk will not go beyond the personhaving a bad time. But, exposing oneself to a real traffic situation without safety guarantees[47], in a case of amaxophobia, is recklessness, as well as negligence.

At present, there are some sensitivities and discrepancies of criteria about the possible professional intrusiveness when road safety training teachers offer to treat fear of driving. As already mentioned, if the fear is rational, and is due to lack of experience, because the person has lost practice after years without driving, then the road safety training professional is the right person to accompany individually the person who requires a reinforcement in his practical learning (it is not a phobia).

But, in the case of amaxophobia, where the fear is irrational, we are dealing with drivers who drive the vehicle in a calm and safe manner, demonstrating knowledge, skill and ability,as long as they do not enter their particular and specific con-text of fear (driving on the highway, or through a tunnel, or at night, or on roads without shoulders..., depending on the

case). It is clear then that these drivers do not need further training to increase their driving skills. The solution, for these

---

[47] We consider that a guarantee of safety in live exposure, for cases of amaxophobia, is obtained when the actual exposure is carried out in a vehicle equipped with dual control by a driver training instructor.

cases, is not to subject the amaxophobic to a process whose only objective is to do practices that they do not need. Phobias must be treated by a professional psychologist or psychiatrist in an authorized and legally accredited center.

The point is that in secondary amaxophobia there comes a time when the amaxophobic has to be exposed live (real circulation)... And, at that moment, the psychology professional usually has neither the practical knowledge nor the adapted vehicle with dual control that offers the appropriate safety conditions, so that the situation is no more dangerous than asimple car ride.

And, if we talk about primary amaxophobia[48] . The psychologist alone cannot advance in the treatment, since the person has to overcome his amaxophobia while learning to drive. The situation, if possible, in this case, is much more complex, since the teaching-learning process of driving is doomed to failure, because the teacher, no matter how much will and effort he puts into it, does not know professionally the psychological techniques and strategies for his student to overcome his phobia and thus overcome the psychological barriers that prevent him from advancing in his learning to drive.

In this case, what options do we have?

In my opinion, I believe that there are three possible alternatives: (a) the psychologist, in addition to being a psychology professional, is a road safety training teacher and has an authorized vehicle with dual controls (clutch, brake and accelerator); (b) the road safety training teachers study psycho- logy and can therefore legally treat phobias and in turn ac- company their patients safely during the actual exposure, and; (c) **psychologists and road safety training teachersform a professional tandem with the aim of maximizingtreatment results and thereby achieving optimal safetyin the actual exposure**.

At this point, we see that: both for primary amaxophobia and for the live exposure phase of secondary amaxophobia, the

[48] Primary amaxophobia (fear of driving in pre-drivers) 19% of pre-drivers, of the latter 15% are women and 4% men. For more information see article: Sánchez, S. (2012). Assessment of fear of driving or amaxophobia in pre- drivers. *Securitas Vialis*. Retrieved from https://www.infona.pl/re- source/bwmetal.element.springer-5719ff30-faa4-332c-b36f-a9a1ac3b4435

ideal situation requires that the road safety teacher, advised by his or her psychologist of reference, knows the steps of the psychological treatment of each case that they are treating together. In turn, the psychologist has to receive from the road safety teacher all the relevant information thatallows him/her to know the evolution of the practical process,the moments where anxiety peaks occur, how the patient orclient solves those critical moments, etc. etc.

I think that each professional, within his or her area of expertise, can help to achieve the goal shared and desired by both... To help the person suffering from amaxophobia to overcome his or her fear of driving. I also believe that this isthe best formula to achieve an optimal, holistic and safe treatment, since both figures separately and alone will achieve, atmost, a partial result, since the intervention will lack that partthat complements the process.

For some years now, in our CFORP center in Viladecans (Barcelona), we have been giving courses on "How to teach how to overcome amaxophobia". These seminars have been addressed to psychology professionals and road safetyteachers. In no case have we intended that some of them acquire the competences of the others, simply our purpose has been, and still is, to establish a bridge between professionals so that each of them knows what their functions are, what is their area of intervention and how working together:one can complement their shortcomings with the contributionof the other and vice versa.

Nor do I want to conclude this text without referring to some circumstances and conditions that would be good to consider.

a) Although the techniques and resources that I have shared with you are tools that can be assumed to be generic, you have to keep in mind that it is unlikely that you will find two cases alike, since all people aredifferent: in our way of perceiving, learning, responding..., so it is essential to adapt each of the resources presented here to each particular subject, to their idiosyncrasy and their current circumstances.

b) In the words of Carl Rogers, to facilitate success, trust and empathy must be promoted. You have to believein the person and the treatment. If we don't believe that it can work It won't work! No matter how much we follow step by step what has been read so far.

Before closing and saying goodbye to you, whether you are a person who suffers from amaxophobia, or any other type of phobia, and have been curious to know more about irrational fear and the anxiety that accompanies it, or if you are a psychology or psychiatry professional who has been interested in investigating or delving into other possible ways of seeing, being and being, in relation to this area of knowledge,I want to express my gratitude for reading this far and for having accompanied me in this experience. In any case, it ismy wish: not to have disappointed you. And, my wish: That you have found in this reading the answers you had hoped tofind.

Recommended bibliography

Bandler, R. (1997). *Magic in action.* Editorial Sirio: Málaga.

From Nardone, G. (2003). *Más allá del miedo: Superar rápidamente las fobias, las obsesiones y el pánico.* Paidós Ibérica: Barcelona.

Ellis, A. and Grieger, R. (2003). *Rational-emotive therapy manual.* Plaza edition: Bilbao.

Festinger, L. (1957). A theory of cognitive dissonance. Stanford, CA: Stanford University Press.

Grinder, J. and Bandler, R. (1993). *Trance-formate:practicalcourseof hypnosis with neurolinguistic programming.* Gaia ediciones: Madrid.

Hawkins, P. (2007). *Hypnosis and stress.* Editorial Desclée de Brouwer: Bilbao.

Martín, Á. and Vázquez, C. (2005*). When I meet captain Hook: (not) hooking me. Practice ingestaltpsychotherapy.* Editorial Desclée de Brouwer: Bilbao.

Pérez, E. (2005). *Amaxophobia or fear of driving.* Mapfre Institute of Road Safety.

Ready, R., Barton, K. and Guix, X. (2003). *PNL for dummies: Educate your unconscious and make your desires come true.* Plaza edition: Barcelona.

Rogers, C. (1972). *Client-centered psychotherapy.* Buenos Aires: Paidós

Sánchez, S. and Sánchez J. (2009-2019). How to teach to overcome amaxophobia. Printed on Amazon.

Sánchez, S. (2011). Validation of a brief questionnaire for the assessment of fear of driving in pre-drivers. *SecuritasVialis,* 9, 37-52.

Sánchez, S. (2012). Assessment of fear of driving or amaxophobia in pre-drivers. *Securitas Vialis*.

Sánchez, S. (2014). Evaluation of the effectiveness of a program designed to overcome fear of driving or amaxophobia. *Securitas Vialis*.

Sanchez S. (2019). You decide, you change, you live. Printed on Amazon.

Sanchez S. (2020). How to overcome phobias. Printed on Amazon.

Torrebadella, P. (1997). How to develop emotional intelligence. RBA. Ediciones de Librerías: Barcelona.

Vázquez, M.I. (2001). *Relaxation and breathing techniques*. Plaza edition: Madrid.